DANIELS AND FISHER

DENVER'S BEST
PLACE TO SHOP

MARK A. BARNHOUSE

THE
History
PRESS

Published by The History Press
Charleston, SC
www.historypress.net

Front cover: Author's collection.
Back cover, top: *Bob Rhodes Collection*; *center*: *Denver Public Library, Western History Collection*; *bottom*: *Ron and Judy Proctor Collection*.

First published 2015

Manufactured in the United States

ISBN 978.1.62619.923.1

Library of Congress Control Number: 2015949883

Notice: The information in this book is true and complete to the best of our knowledge. It is offered without guarantee on the part of the author or The History Press. The author and The History Press disclaim all liability in connection with the use of this book.

For my sister, Sandra Ellen Barnhouse, a long-ago May-D&F employee.

CONTENTS

ACKNOWLEDGEMENTS

Many kind people contributed in both tangible and intangible ways to this book. I am particularly indebted to former May-D&F vice-president Robert "Bob" Rhodes, who graciously shared both memories and photographs; Alan Golin Gass, FAIA, who shared photographs and wonderful stories of his time working with I.M. Pei; Richard Hentzell, the driving force behind the Daniels and Fisher Tower's continuing vitality in recent years, who enlightened me regarding some obscure points; and Ron and Judy Proctor, whose extensive collection of Daniels and Fisher memorabilia and knowledge of the store's past made this a more interesting book. I am grateful to the following individuals who shared memories or photos or helped in other ways: Robert and Kristen Autobee, Sandra E. Barnhouse, Regina Bullock, Serena Elavia and the *Atlantic*, Carol Hiller, Becky LeJeune, Dr. Thomas J. Noel, Heather Ormsby, Richard Rhodes, Suzanne Ryan, Jodi Sokup of Clocktower Events, Shantelle Stephens and Izzy Vera. The always-helpful people at the Denver Public Library Western History and Genealogy Collection were invaluable (in particular, Abby Hoverstock and Coi Drummond-Gehrig), as was the fine staff at the Stephen H. Hart Library at History Colorado (in particular, Melissa VanOtterloo). Thanks, too, to Jaime Bourassa of the Missouri History Museum, Library and Research Center. At The History Press, editor Krista Slavicek was both helpful and patient. As always, thank you for everything you do, Matt.

Introduction
TWO LANDMARK STORES

This book tells the story of two Denver department stores that together served residents of the Mile High City and all Coloradoans for thirteen decades. Daniels and Fisher was born in 1864, when Denver was only six years old; its successor store, May-D&F, began operations in 1958, after May Company (founded in Leadville, Colorado, in 1877) bought Daniels and Fisher and merged the older store's operations with its own. It continued operating as May-D&F until a corporate reshuffling in 1993 resulted in its name vanishing from the Denver landscape.

These two stores, one succeeding the other, are united by not only the lineage of their names but also by the architectural approach they took to their buildings: both Daniels and Fisher and May-D&F built landmarks on Denver's Sixteenth Street that made shopping a special event. Their competitors (Denver Dry Goods, Joslin's and, in earlier years, Golden Eagle) were all successful and respectable merchants, but their buildings were relatively utilitarian, designed to house goods but not make a mark on the cityscape.

Roughly resembling Venice's Campanile di San Marco, the slender Daniels and Fisher Tower occupies a plot of ground only 40 feet square and rises 330 feet (375 feet with flagpole) from the corner of the Sixteenth Street Mall and Arapahoe Street. To a person unacquainted with the tower's history, it would seem an architectural folly—not connected to any larger building, its small footprint makes it appear as though it couldn't have been built for any useful purpose. The design is classical: a stone base, a buff-colored brick shaft and a pyramidal crown capped by a cupola. Near the top, clock faces point in four directions; just below the clock, columns and arches handsomely frame inset balconies. Over the door, a plaque proclaims "Erected by William Cooke Daniels MCMXI." The tallest building between Chicago and San Francisco when built, it reigned over Denver's skyline for more than four decades after its 1911 debut. No mere folly, the tower not only served as a symbol of the fine department store to which it was once attached but also marked Denver's maturation from frontier outpost into a big city.

Several blocks up the Sixteenth Street Mall, at the corner with Tremont Street, another landmark once stood that, in a later era, also signaled Denver's transformation from provincial burg into worldly city. May-D&F opened in 1958 as "the first completely new major department store in the country to be built in the heart of a downtown area since World War II."[1] It appeared at a time when it was clear that suburban branches were the coming trend, although perhaps no one quite yet envisioned the proliferation of enclosed malls that would lead to closure of most downtown flagship stores, eventually including this one. This landmark store was not the artistic vision of a second-generation merchant prince like William Cooke Daniels, but rather the urbane creation of a very different sort of man, one of the twentieth century's most colorful master builders: William Zeckendorf. Based in New York City, his Webb & Knapp, Inc. specialized in civilization-enhancing projects—Zeckendorf truly saw himself as "making a worthwhile contribution to the future of man."[2] For his May-D&F-anchored Courthouse Square project, he commissioned his architect, I.M. Pei, to create something special, and Pei did: a 400,000-square-foot department store, clad in golden aluminum, with a thin-shell concrete, glass-walled "hyperbolic paraboloid" in front serving as its glorious entrance. Adjoining the paraboloid, Pei designed a sunken plaza, used in winter as a Rockefeller Center–style urban ice-skating rink. Across Court Place, a vast hotel complemented the store, paraboloid and plaza, the assemblage creating just the worthwhile contribution to Denver that Zeckendorf had promised. When May-D&F opened, it adopted the moniker "Shopping Wonder of the West," and for a time, it was.

There is more to the story than landmark buildings or the commerce that took place inside them. By their very nature, department stores are about people. William Bradley Daniels—conservative, proper Episcopalian that he was—proved perfectly capable of letting his heart rule his head when he met the alluring Donna Madixxa. His son, William Cooke Daniels, raised in luxury and given every advantage, was not content to live as a pampered

Daniels and Fisher after the 1911 completion of its landmark tower. *Thomas J. Noel Collection/Library of Congress.*

millionaire but gave of himself, furthering the cause of science, volunteering to serve his country and building his city a token of his esteem that is still with us today. A third William, Zeckendorf, sought to wake up sleepy Denver, wrest it into the twentieth century and perhaps make a dollar at the

May-D&F, centerpiece of Courthouse Square, circa 1960. *Denver Public Library, Western History Collection.*

same time. William Garrett Fisher, David May, Charles MacAllister Willcox, Cicely Banner Daniels, Florence Martin, Joe Ross, Carl Sandell, Mary Alice Fitzgerald, Bob Rhodes—some well-known names, and some not so well-known, but each of them contributes their human stories to this narrative.

Daniels and Fisher was Denver's pioneer store, a homegrown institution that never lost sight of its western roots even as it aspired to put Denver on the map with its splendid tower. May-D&F succeeded Daniels and Fisher, and although controlled by a parent company one thousand miles away, for many years it embodied a "Colorado" personality—May Company's roots were in the state, too, after all. These were Colorado stores for Colorado people, and Colorado took pride in them.

Part I

DENVER'S MAGNIFICENT STORE

Chapter 1
PIONEER MERCHANTS

A tiny puff of wind blew over the sun-baked prairie, tossing the shriveled, tumbling weeds against the wheels of an oxen drawn wagon as it slowly jolted across the plain. And that, as the story-books say, was how it all began.[3]

All Wool and a Yard Wide

Daniels and Fisher founder William Bradley Daniels was born in 1825, in the tiny western New York village of Friendship, Allegany County, where he attended school with two other boys who would, like him, figure prominently in Colorado history: future senator Henry Moore Teller and Henry's brother, Willard. Upon reaching adulthood in the mid-1840s, Daniels moved to New York City, where he spent several years learning the retail trade. There he met a Chicago merchant, Henry Potwin, who planted in him the idea of heading west, where opportunities were said to be exceptional, and for a number of years, Daniels conducted a thriving dry goods business in Iowa City, Iowa, in partnership with Potwin. Perennially ambitious, he began investing in other businesses in other towns, eventually opening a second establishment in Leavenworth, Kansas, a dry goods store in partnership with a man named Daniel Azro Millington. Daniels married, but his first wife died about a year after the wedding; in 1860, he married Elizabeth P. Knox, the second Mrs. Daniels.[4]

Meanwhile, six hundred miles west of Leavenworth, a city was busy being born. The discovery of gold in the South Platte River in the summer of 1858 led to the birth later that year of a town near the confluence of that stream and a quiet little watercourse called Cherry Creek. Or rather, it led to the birth of three towns: Auraria, on the southwest bank of Cherry Creek; St. Charles, on its northeast bank; and another, founded in the same spot by a claim jumper named William H. Larimer Jr. A "veteran town promoter" from Leavenworth, Larimer took advantage of the absence of the St. Charles founders, who had gone back east for the winter. Possibly seeking political protection for his questionable claim, Larimer named his town for the governor of Kansas Territory (of which his town site was then part), James William Denver. Although Denver had actually resigned by this time, Denver City soon became well known, and when, in 1860, Auraria, Denver and Highland (on the west bank of the South Platte, also founded by Larimer) decided to merge, it was the former governor's name that stuck.[5]

The imprecisely named 1859 "Pike's Peak Gold Rush" (which occurred many miles north of that mountain), attracting thousands of prospectors looking for easy wealth, generated a need for a place where they could obtain supplies and advice and exchange their gold dust. Denver, although it had competitors, soon became the primary hub for this economic activity, thanks to the efforts of city boosters such as Larimer, William Gilpin and William Newton Byers, who had founded Colorado's first newspaper, the *Rocky Mountain News*, on April 17, 1859. Byers, prone to embellishment ("a little bright perhaps" is how he characterized his stories decades later), did his best to ensure that people would come.[6]

It may have been Byers's articles, often reprinted in other newspapers, which piqued Daniels's attention in 1864. Whatever the spark, that year he sent his sister's husband, William R. Kenyon, to the young city to reconnoiter. Kenyon's report was favorable, so Daniels sent him back with a wagonload of assorted goods to set up a new branch (in some accounts written decades later, Kenyon was accompanied by a junior store partner, John Eckhart). This was after a discussion with Millington, who was skeptical of Denver's chances and wanted no part of a business venture there. Daniels therefore funded it entirely himself.[7]

Kenyon arrived in October, part of the first wagon train to arrive since May (fears of troubles with Arapahoe and Cheyenne First Peoples had hampered travel). His stock, including picks, shovels and miner's boots, along with "heavy, coarse" clothing, was meant to appeal to miners and prospectors. On October 6, he opened W.B. Daniels & Company in a narrow storefront at F (now Fifteenth) and Blake Streets, in the Fillmore Block, facing Blake. This location was then near the center of Denver's retail trade, which ran mostly along F Street between Larimer and Wazee, and down the named streets on either side of it.[8]

Kenyon eventually returned home, and Daniels sent out John M. Eckhart, making him a partner. This necessitated the first of many name changes: W.B. Daniels & Company became Daniels and Eckhart & Company. Eckhart, despite the high rates (from twelve and a half to twenty-five cents per pound) paid for freight across the prairie, decided to risk stocking higher-quality goods. He had noticed that the city's many gamblers were "always well dressed in fine, white linen and handsome, black broadcloth," and felt he could make money courting them as customers.[9]

Eckhart's instincts were apparently quite sound, because trade began to grow to the point that the small Blake Street space was soon inadequate. He rented a second storefront (keeping the first) two blocks away on Larimer Street. This one-story building was not on the corner with F/Fifteenth but near it (today, this block is Writer Square, a 1981 commercial/residential development). Eckhart split the merchandise: the new branch specialized in carpets and other household items, while the original store sold men's and women's clothing, along with dry goods associated with apparel: bolt goods, ribbons, laces, millinery and countless other items necessary for the proper Victorian wardrobe. Daniels and Eckhart cultivated a solid reputation, selling quality goods that were "all wool and a yard wide," a phrase that would be associated with the store for decades. Another slogan (a circular one, certainly) the merchants were fond of using was "If it is good, we have it. If we have it, it is good."[10]

In the fall of 1869, the five-year-old firm moved the one-story Larimer store into a new three-story building at 390 Larimer (390 was the designation under the old system; it was later renumbered 1548, which places it where today's Writer Square office building stands). In its new home, the firm became known especially for its fine stock of carpets. On the lower end, a buyer could pay fifty cents to one dollar and fifty cents per yard for a type known as "ingrain," or, for those with more to spend, fine Brussels, Axminsters and Wiltons could be had, some for as much as fifteen dollars per yard.[11]

About this time, an incident occurred that became legendary among the store's employees, one that would often appear in later publicity materials. A store buyer, either in a fit of enthusiasm or perhaps just inept with numbers, ordered a huge shipment of trouser buttons, far more than the store could

Larimer Street between Fifteenth and Sixteenth was home to the first branch of W.B. Daniels (circa 1866), visible two doors to the right of the post office. *Denver Public Library, Western History Collection.*

Daniels & Eckhart occupied three-story quarters at 390 Larimer in 1869; here the firm became Daniels and Fisher & Company. *Denver Public Library, Western History Collection.*

hope to sell in a year ("hundreds of great gross," as a store history described it). Daniels was unhappy with the costly mistake, so the resourceful buyer figured out a profitable way to dispose of the buttons. In those days, gambling in Colorado was unrestricted, and keno parlors were popular. The buyer took a sample button to a nearby keno parlor and soon sold the entire lot to the proprietor to be used as keno counters. [12]

The following year, 1870, Daniels's only child was born in Iowa City, where he had continued in business, and where his sister, Sarah M. Kenyon, still lived. He and Elizabeth christened their son William Cooke Daniels; as a child, he was known as Willie.

Enter Fisher

The year 1872 brought a second name change to the eight-year-old firm. William Garrett Fisher (like Daniels from New York state), who had clerked at Daniels's Iowa City store, had arrived in Denver two years earlier to assist the busy Eckhart. Fisher, twenty years younger than Daniels (so just twenty-six years old in 1870) and a Union veteran of the Civil War, was a merchant to his core. A story, perhaps apocryphal, told of his wartime trading with the Confederate enemy, exchanging Northern apples for Southern tobacco. [13]

Fisher worked long, hard days, as the store kept late hours to capture the trade of those who were otherwise busy during the daytime. On most days, it stayed open until 10:00 p.m. and sometimes wouldn't close until midnight. Although he boarded at American House (located at Sixteenth and Blake Streets), the city's finest hotel in those years, many nights he slept in the store after working an eighteen-hour day. In a letter to his mother, he wrote, "Business here is much greater than in Iowa…our sales amount to from $400 to $1,000 a day." Although he didn't show resentment, he continued, "Mr. Eckhart drives his help even harder than Mr. Daniels ever did." But Daniels, managing the firm from afar, had his eyes on Fisher; every Monday, he required the young man to write him with a digest of the previous week's trade. By May 1870 (he had arrived only in March), he was able to tell his mother, "The business is almost entirely in my charge, and as it is the most successful business in the territory it proves that as Mr. Daniels says, I have a good deal of business capacity." [14]

Work was difficult, not only for Fisher (who claimed he did "not get over 5½ hours sleep and [had not] one free moment all day long"). Clerks would be hired and soon quit due to the heavy volume. "Goods is [*sic*] arriving daily, from one to twenty cases—and each must be marked before going to bed. We had 13 different clerks since August 1," Fisher wrote on September 13, 1870, "and only three have stayed."[15]

Fisher showed such great promise that when Eckhart in 1872 decided to become a silent partner (retaining an ownership share for a few more years), Daniels made Fisher his new partner, and Daniels and Fisher & Company was born. Fisher, with his junior ownership stake, was busier than ever. He told his mother he had to "write up all my orders every night and send them to Mr. Daniels. We buy anything we think we can sell and the credit of the house is good for many hundred thousand dollars."[16]

The *Rocky Mountain News* would later praise Fisher (an important advertiser, of course) for his "business experience and tact, his pleasant personal and social address, and his sterling integrity," which was necessary to lead a store that "has now scarcely a rival in the west, either in the elegance or excellence of its stock, the extent of its sales, or the esteem and popularity in which it is held." It was good for Daniels that he had such an able partner running the show in Denver. With his interests in Leavenworth and Iowa City, and kept busy running his New York wholesale firm (Daniels, Cohen & Company) and buying stock for his Denver store, he overworked himself to the point of exhaustion. His doctor prescribed rest, which Daniels took as an extended European vacation; he did not make his full-time residence in Denver until 1878.[17]

Chapter 2

CARRIAGE TRADE

The people of Denver take great pride and feel a personal interest in this old pioneer establishment. It has grown apace with the city and its population, till now it ranks in character and standard with the first houses of Marshall Field of Chicago, Arnold Constable & Co. and Seigel, Cooper & Co. of New York, and Jordan, Marsh & Co. of Boston...[18]

THE STEWART'S OF THE WEST

The national depression that followed the financial Panic of 1873 did not affect young Denver in quite the extreme way eastern cities were impacted. Perhaps it was the city's relative isolation (the first rail line had arrived only in 1871), or more likely, that its economy was so closely tied to thriving extractive industries, but by 1875, the business at Daniels and Fisher was so strong that Fisher knew another move was necessary. Daniels's initial Denver venture, followed by a branch and then a larger one, were gambles that had paid off handsomely. In 1875, Fisher decided to gamble again, buying two lots on the eastern corner of Sixteenth and Lawrence Streets and commissioning a two-story building (plus basement), 50 feet wide by 125 feet deep, which opened the following year.[19]

This was a canny move—Larimer had by then supplanted Fifteenth as the city's primary commercial thoroughfare, but some more fashionable shops were beginning to cluster one block away on Lawrence Street. Fisher had no way of knowing that Sixteenth Street would eventually become Denver's primary shopping promenade, but his choice was fortuitous; had he chosen a corner on Fifteenth or Seventeenth, the history of Daniels and Fisher might have turned out differently. In the beginning, however, it was not at all clear that Sixteenth Street was to become important, so the store's front, faced in impressive dressed stone with large windows, faced Lawrence. The Sixteenth Street side was built of humbler red brick, the most common building material in the city. However, architect Frank E. Edbrooke wisely placed the entrance on the corner to capture the trade from two directions.

The new store took off, and in a year, Daniels and Fisher decided to sell the original Blake Street store to its manager so the firm could concentrate on its new location exclusively. Growing rapidly, by 1878, it employed between forty and fifty sales clerks, as well as nearly one hundred women who manufactured ladies' clothing, undergarments and other items. Taking advantage of volume buying, the firm had built a thriving wholesale department, operating from the basement, supplying smaller stores in Colorado and neighboring states with Daniels and Fisher wares. Upstairs on the second floor was the carpet department, with $100,000 in annual sales (approximately $2.3 million in today's dollars), and an upholstery shop.[20]

Daniels and Fisher at Sixteenth and Lawrence Streets, circa 1881, with Skinner Brothers & Wright under construction at left. *Denver Public Library, Western History Collection.*

BANDEAUX, CURLS, FRIZZES, PUFFS, SCOLLOPS.

An early advertisement for both wholesale and retail operations. *Thomas J. Noel collection.*

Two stories and a basement soon proved inadequate for a booming business, and Fisher decided to add two more floors. By the time the new four-story emporium—now with dressed stone on both the Lawrence and Sixteenth Street façades—opened in 1879, Denver boosters were becoming fond of comparing Daniels and Fisher to the most famous store in America at that time, A.T. Stewart and Company of New York City.[21]

By the time this "Stewart's of the West" filled four floors, it employed 250 men and women and had sales in the millions annually. Fashionable Denver women could buy not only their carpets and dry goods there but also myriad imported items in silk, velvet, lace and other luxurious materials. Men could buy suits (including ones made of fine Scottish or English tweed) or more prosaic items: underwear, duck clothing for outdoor use, woolen shirts, hats, gloves, shoes and boots. The firm manufactured many goods in-house, providing employment, saving freight costs and, in a day when "globalization" was not yet even a word, keeping Denver's money in Denver.[22]

Wholesale Department sample room, circa 1907. *Denver Public Library, Western History Collection.*

That same year of 1879, Daniels sensed another business opportunity in the mining boomtown of Leadville. Others had already become rich, or at least very successful, in the "Cloud City" (elevation 10,521 feet), including Horace Austin Warner Tabor, who was then building Denver's most impressive business structure, the five-story Tabor Block, just one block down Sixteenth Street from Daniels and Fisher at Larimer. Also by this time, another pioneer merchant, David May, was conducting a thriving trade in Leadville. Daniels announced to Fisher that he was going to Leadville "to prospect," but not for silver. After finding a site at Third Street and Harrison Avenue, near the new Tabor Opera House, Daniels found a third partner for their high country venture, Joel W. Smith. The Daniels, Fisher and Smith store prospered for several years, with Smith coming to own 100 percent of it after Daniels's death. Inventory came from Daniels and Fisher's booming wholesale division.[23]

That business, which had originated in the basement, moved up to the new fourth floor in 1879 and, when a fifth floor was added in 1893, came to occupy it as well. Denver, the largest city in the Rocky Mountain West, was the logical supply point for a vast territory, and Daniels and Fisher supplied smaller retailers not only all over Colorado but also in

Harrison Avenue, Leadville, with Daniels, Fisher & Smith visible at left. *Denver Public Library, Western History Collection.*

By 1907, the store had added a fifth floor, expanded farther down Lawrence Street and opened up the Sixteenth Street side (right) with large plate-glass windows. *Denver Public Library, Western History Collection.*

Utah, Wyoming, Idaho, Montana, Nebraska, South Dakota, New Mexico, Arizona and Nevada. Traveling salesmen plied the hinterlands bearing wholesale catalogues, taking orders from small-town merchants. During the store's first four decades, the wholesale division was by far the more profitable part of the firm.[24]

The retail side continued to grow, however, along with Denver's population, thanks to Daniels and Fisher's reputation for high-quality merchandise. The store bought adjacent lots along Lawrence Street and added on to the original building in 1888 and again in 1898, in the materials and style of the 1876 original.[25]

THE CUSTOMER IS ALWAYS RIGHT

The Panic of 1893, which devastated Colorado's economy, certainly impacted Daniels and Fisher, but the firm kept up a confident appearance (building a fifth floor that year visibly demonstrated that undaunted attitude) and made it through the panic and severe economic depression that followed.[26] Denver banks, so closely tied to Colorado's mining and smelting industries, largely collapsed, with seven closing their doors on one bleak day, July 18, 1893, and several more failing shortly thereafter; the repeal of the Sherman Silver Purchase Act of 1890, which had propped up Colorado's silver economy, followed in October, sealing the coffin on silver mining.[27] Denver newspapers in that hot, tense month of July were filled with advertisements from over-extended merchants who depended on steady cash flow, screaming "MUST RAISE CASH" in large type, followed by descriptions of spectacular "sacrifice" bargains to be had. While Daniels and Fisher weathered the storm, not all stores made it; the most spectacular failure occurred several blocks up Sixteenth Street, at California Street, where the new, three-story home of M.J. McNamara Dry Goods Company was soon emptied of its goods and padlocked by the sheriff. The following year, two Denver businessmen, Dennis Sheedy and Charles Kountze, bought the building and reopened it as Denver Dry Goods Company, a store that would eventually rival Daniels and Fisher in size and prestige.

The glory days of "the Denver" were still in the future, however; in the 1890s, Daniels and Fisher still held sway as the largest retailer in Colorado. As described in a contemporaneous issue of the *Rocky Mountain Herald*, the grandest store in the city was organized around an atrium (likely introduced

The Lawrence Street addition featured an atrium, helping illuminate dark corners. *Denver Public Library, Western History Collection.*

with the 1888 addition, although no sources explicitly say so), lit in the daytime by a "massive skylight," allowing every floor to receive natural light. It was richly elegant, with "no shabby fixtures, no neglected corners, no dark aisles as detract from most stores."[28]

Upon entering, a shopper was greeted with dry goods, "a wealth of stuffs piled up or displayed on every hand…aisle after aisle of silks and dress goods and laces, and linens, and domestics, and bed clothing, and flannels, and cloths, and gloves, and underwear, and handkerchiefs, and notions, and trimmings, and linings," and so on. The second floor featured ladies' clothing, "imported costumes, exquisite wraps from Paris, beautiful gowns, coats and jackets from London and Berlin, costly furs, tailor-made suits, and whatever else constitutes elegance in women's apparel." On this floor were also a children's clothing department, millinery, a department filled "with bronzes and marbles, china and porcelain," "bric-a-brac" and other *objets d'art*, along with "the most charming tea room in Denver," and a "ladies' balcony" furnished with easy chairs and writing desks, where women could meet friends or take a break from shopping. On the third floor were Daniels and Fisher's famous carpets, "standing up in serried ranks," along with "exquisite stuffs for hangings and draperies," and a furniture department. The fourth and fifth floors were still given over to the wholesale operation and clothing manufacturing and tailoring, while in the basement were departments for chinaware, glassware, toys, luggage and other household goods.

Keeping the store running was a general manager, J.M. Fleming, who had been recruited from Marshall Field & Company in Chicago, Stewart's rival as the leading American department store. The twenty-five departments answered to him but were structured almost as individual businesses, each with a profit and loss statement, its own buyers and a strict hierarchy. Serving on each floor were floorwalkers, who directed customers to departments and handled problems. Clerks of both sexes ranked below floorwalkers, not only selling merchandise but also constantly straightening displays (not unlike modern retail workers). Below clerks, cash boys and girls carried money to central cashiers, took purchased items to the wrapping department and then brought them back to waiting customers, along with the customer's change. Behind the scenes were bookkeepers, night watchmen, receiving clerks, window dressers and others who kept all parts of the machine running. If customers preferred not to carry the goods home, a fleet of horse-drawn wagons provided prompt delivery to any city address.

Also aiding the female shopper was a new innovation: credit. In that more patriarchal time, women often did not have much cash of their own and were dependent on their fathers or husbands for it. Men were reluctant to give them too much at one time, so Daniels and Fisher (similar to department stores in other cities) began extending credit to women who were known to have the ability to pay. Unlike modern credit cards, which allow for balances carried forward, these accounts were due and payable each month when statements were mailed to their husbands.[29]

Sales people did not exert strong pressure to buy. Daniels, Fisher and their upper management trained employees to welcome all visitors, whether they bought anything or not, and to not apply pressure so that a shopper felt forced into buying something that perhaps she could not afford. This set the store in great contrast to smaller specialty shops that sold just one kind of product, such as millinery, dresses or shoes, where no one could browse anonymously and where clerks earned their pay primarily from commission. Also, Daniels and Fisher adopted a policy that "the customer is always right," similar to that of department stores elsewhere. While it was Chicago's Marshall Field who coined the famous phrase "give the lady what she wants," Daniels and Fisher's policy was essentially the same.[30]

There were, of course, a number of Denver women who could afford just about anything the store had available. Best remembered of these was millionaire Tabor's second wife, Elizabeth McCourt "Baby Doe" Tabor,

The first-floor dry goods department, circa 1902. Perhaps some of these men had served Baby Doe Tabor. *Denver Public Library, Western History Collection.*

whom he had married after scandalously divorcing his first wife, Augusta. The second Mrs. Tabor would arrive in a black barouche, drawn by four white horses, outside the store's carriage entrance on Lawrence Street. She would instruct the doorman who greeted her at curbside to "send out the silk man." Some minutes later, the head of the silks department would arrive loaded with bolts of cloth, from which Baby Doe would select materials to be sent to her dressmaker.[31]

The *Rocky Mountain Herald* piece that described the store's wonders summarized the business philosophy of Daniels and Fisher: "The house seduously [*sic*] avoids notoriety, and manages its affairs with conservative dignity." There was a very good reason for the store to avoid notoriety, as the next chapter will show.

Chapter 3
A MELODRAMA

I am in ecstasy with the hopes and prospect of meeting you this evening. I will call at ½ past 8 and if all is right, leave the lower part of the middle window blind partly open—of your chamber...expect your own husband at the time mentioned or as soon after as the sign is given. Prepare a sweet kiss for me.
Your Loving Pa Pa[32]

LILYON

With plentiful money flowing in from Leadville, the 1880s was a boom decade for Denver. William Bradley Daniels, now a millionaire and leading citizen, would remain so despite the rather sensational cast his life assumed during this period. His beloved Elizabeth, who had borne his only son, had suffered from tuberculosis and died in 1881, before young Willie reached puberty. After a relatively short mourning period, the father did what many men who were past the middle stages of their lives do in a similar situation: he began to look around.

In 1882, he found what he thought he was looking for, in the person of a much younger woman, Lilyon Donna Abbott (née Beardsley). Born in Madrid to a Spanish mother and an American father, Lilyon, according to later accounts, had classically Castilian features, with a fair complexion, deep brown hair and eyes "that flash forth beauty in darts capable of stirring the heart of the coldest man."[33] She was but two generations removed from aristocracy—her grandfather was Maria Josefa Maguil, the Count Madixxa. She had come to Denver in 1881 at the advice of her sister Christine, who was working in the Daniels and Fisher cloak department. At twenty-seven years of age, she was a recent divorcée with no alimony but with a degree from Boston University School of Oratory and an intention of using her education to make a living.

Hearing from Christine that Denver was flush with cash, she came west to establish an elocution school. She expected the *nouveaux riches* would want to polish their personalities to go along with their new lives as leading citizens. Unlike most elocution teachers of the time, she would aim her lessons at husbands rather than wives, because she knew that men had greater insecurities when it came to public speaking. She met Daniels through Christine, and he, concerned about his boy's none-too-strong lungs, soon enrolled Willie in her classes to benefit from her deep-breathing lessons. Daniels fell in love with Lilyon, and on July 8, 1882, a whirlwind romance turned into a marriage.

Left: Lilyon Beardsley Daniels, also known as Donna Madixxa, the third wife of William Bradley Daniels. *History Colorado.*

Right: William Bradley Daniels, late in life. *History Colorado.*

William B. Daniels built this mansion at 1422 Curtis Street for Donna Madixxa, but she never lived in it. *Denver Public Library, Western History Collection.*

This is not, of course, the best known of Denver's May-December romances of the 1880s. It was "Silver King" Horace Tabor, who, being smitten with young divorcée Elizabeth McCourt Doe ("Baby Doe," mentioned in chapter 2), divorced Augusta, his wife of twenty-seven years, and married his much-younger paramour in an 1883 ceremony in Washington, D.C., during Tabor's brief stint as a replacement U.S. senator. Later, Tabor lost his millions, but Baby Doe stayed by him and held on to the Matchless Mine in Leadville after he died, until she froze to death there in 1935. That story has been told so often (in articles and books; as a Hollywood movie, *Silver Dollar*; and even as an opera, Douglas Moore's *The Ballad of Baby Doe*) that it is widely familiar; the story of Mr. and Mrs. William Bradley Daniels, though once filling newspaper columns, is much less well known today. In its time, it was nearly as sensational as the Tabor saga.

Returning from their honeymoon, William and Lilyon took up residence in Daniels's Curtis Park residence on Champa Street. As he normally spent little time in Denver, it was not overly fancy, comprising one half of a duplex. He had plans for his new life, however: he would build Lilyon an ornate mansion on Denver's "Millionaire's Row," at 1422 Curtis Street (later the site of the Mountain States Telephone and Telegraph Building).

Donna Madixxa

Trouble soon commenced. As a widower, Daniels had lived only with his coachman and housekeeper, a married African American couple named Henry and Annie Mitchell (Willie had been sent to boarding school). When the newlyweds arrived, the new Mrs. Daniels and Mrs. Mitchell soon took a strong dislike to each other. After a particularly ugly confrontation over Annie, Lilyon gave her husband an ultimatum, to choose between his wife and his housekeeper. For his part, Daniels was unhappy with her set of friends, bohemians from the world of the stage; a conservative, Episcopalian Republican, he had little in common with these people. Marriage to a woman half his age, once he had time to think about it, was not altogether wise, and though he still had strong feelings for her, he began to doubt that his sentiments were being fully returned. Refusing to fire Annie, he moved out.[34]

The next day, hearing of his plans to travel to Chicago, Lilyon went to Union Station and boarded his train, hoping to convince him to come back to her. Anxious to avoid a public confrontation, he excused himself to go to the water closet and hopped off just as the train was pulling out. Lilyon didn't realize he was gone until too late; after traveling sixty miles she was forced to wire her sister for money for return fare. She moved in with Christine, while lawyers got to work on a separation agreement. Despite the break, the couple continued to exchange letters, both professing to desire reconciliation but neither willing to compromise.

By early 1883, the separation was legally finalized; about $75,000 ($1.7 million in today's money) in mixed assets became her property, including the Champa Street dwelling but not the under-construction house on Curtis.[35] Both signed the document, but the flame still burned, and he visited her at her sister's home, where they spent a few nights together. They soon quarreled again, however, putting an end to the reconciliation. The new fight may have been about an English "gentleman" who had been seen around town with Lilyon, the self-styled "Lord Roquefort" (whether he was an actual English lord is questionable). Daniels left Denver for an extended business-related stay in New York, and in the fall of 1883, Lilyon followed him there, renting an apartment near the hotel where he always stayed.

Lilyon Daniels then decided to follow another dream, a career on the stage, and began auditioning for parts. As "Miss L. Daniels," she was cast in the role of Bellegentier in *The Stranglers of Paris* at Niblo's Theater, and later joined a company that took that play and others across the country. At some point, she dropped her married name and reverted to her Spanish family name for her theatrical persona: she was now Donna Madixxa.

In January 1885, Madixxa returned to Denver for an engagement in *The Creole*, booked into the Tabor Grand Opera House at Sixteenth and Curtis, just two blocks from Daniels's now-completed mansion and, in another direction, just two blocks from his store. She appeared not under her new stage name, but as Mrs. William B. Daniels, to the discomfort of her husband (who nevertheless watched the show from a curtained, private box). She was not the star, but having many bohemian friends in the city who were all there on opening night, she got such an ovation at the end that the leading lady and man, who had not received such ecstatic applause, quit the company in disgust.[36] The producer then gave the leading role to Madixxa for a short run in Leadville's Tabor Opera House, but the Denver papers' poor reviews of the production preceded it, and the company soon gave up touring. Madixxa returned to Denver, taking rooms at the Windsor Hotel at Eighteenth and Larimer Streets, so she could look after the properties she had received in the separation. Handling her affairs was a purported German aristocrat, Claude von Trotha. She hired new attorneys, one of whom was Daniels's boyhood friend Willard Teller. In February, they presented a lawsuit against Daniels, charging him with desertion and requesting $25,000 per year in alimony. She asserted he had misled her about his net worth at the time of the 1883 separation, and she would claim her share.

Daniels, angered by the lawsuit, decided to strike back. Late one evening after she had filed suit, Madixxa was summoned to the Windsor's lobby, where a young man who had been one of her elocution pupils, and who still admired her, was waiting. An employee of a Denver newspaper, he had notes for an article that was to be published the following day.[37] It was scandalous, accusing her of "breaking all the commandments at once," and it seemed obvious to Madixxa that her husband had had a hand in it. She drafted a letter:

WINDSOR HOTEL.

Mr. Daniels:

I have this moment heard that you have contemplated or have already made defamatory statements about me. You know and I know that they are false and are made for the sole purpose of shielding yourself from the consequences of many wrongs I now suffer at your hands. If such statements have been made or shall be made by you or through your agency—as there is a God above I will kill you the first time I see you.

LILYON DANIELS.
Saturday midnight.
February 28.

She rushed to the Curtis Street mansion, rang the bell and stuffed the letter under the door. A few minutes later, Daniels was awakened. He read the letter, dressed and went immediately to the newspaper office. As a later account put it, "that he instigated the stuff cannot be proved; but he prevented its publication." Daniels told the editor "she would have kept her word. I know that Spaniard!"

The next day, Madixxa bought a gun and Daniels took the first train out of Denver. Not aware that he was gone, Madixxa went to the house and, showing her .38 caliber revolver, told the servants that as the wife of William B. Daniels she was taking possession. Daniels's caretaker, Charles Richards, tried to evict her, but being unsuccessful, he swore out an arrest warrant for her and von Trotha (who had joined her at the house) on a charge of rioting.

At trial, she was acquitted of that charge (it takes at least three to make a riot, Justice George L. Sopris declared), despite pleading guilty. By this time, all of the sordid details of the stormy relationship had come out publicly. In his earlier letters to her, still in love, Daniels had affectionately signed his letters "Pa Pa," and seeking an advantage, Lilyon released them to the press; papers in other cities soon published them, as the "Pa Pa Letters," to Daniels's great embarrassment. Denver opinion largely sided with the prosperous merchant over the tempestuous (and half-foreign) actress. Madixxa's trial for the charge of sending Daniels a written death threat ended in a hung jury, and there was general consensus in the press that the case was not worth pursuing.

Legal wrangling continued, however—they were still officially married, only separated—and Madixxa wanted what she believed was rightfully hers. Daniels was convinced that all her love letters had been lies, designed to lull him into a false sense of her true feelings toward himself. He decided to pursue divorce as the only option left. For grounds, he hired W.A. Wallace, a private investigator, who employed two Windsor Hotel bellhops to spy on her. Wallace easily ingratiated himself with Madixxa, and though she soon figured out that he was working for her husband, she nevertheless kept him around, somehow convinced that he was more loyal to her than to Daniels.

William Garrett Fisher built his Neoclassical mansion at 1600 Logan Street in 1896; it remains standing today. *Denver Public Library, Western History Collection.*

Leaving a $1,500 hotel bill in her wake, in early 1886, she suddenly left Denver for Cheyenne. There, she came down with a case of spinal meningitis and was not expected to live. But she recovered enough to travel and, on the advice of one of Daniels's attorneys, returned to Denver to recuperate. Daniels had finally filed for divorce, and one of his young lawyers, Lafayette Pence (a future congressman) of the office of Charles M. Patterson & Charles S. Thomas, handed her what he said was a receipt to sign for the summons. Wallace was by her bedside and encouraged her to sign it. Madixxa made her mark, and Daniels had what he needed. On March 17, 1886, the court decreed the divorce, on the grounds that Lilyon Beardsley Daniels had committed adultery. She later claimed that she'd been "bereft of reason" when she signed what turned out to be a confession of faithlessness, but there was no going back.

After the divorce, Donna Madixxa left Denver, first for Europe and then eventually resuming her New York stage career. She ultimately lost what she had gained marrying and divorcing Daniels, having placed her Denver property in the hands of a man who lost it through speculating. She later became the mistress of a prominent New York attorney, Lyman E. Warren, according to a divorce suit filed by his wife. Daniels led a much quieter life from then on, but his ex-wife's efforts to obtain a larger financial settlement from him and, later, his son continued for many years, not ceasing until 1898, when a court ruled the divorce lawful.

Chapter 4

MAJOR DANIELS
AND HIS TOWER STORE

*It is Major Daniels' desire that the management be conducted on a basis of
mutual good will and good nature. This attitude on the part of management
is reflected in the atmosphere of the store, where even on the busiest days there
is neither noise nor flurry, so perfect is the oiling of the wheels of this great
mercantile machine. The policy of the store stated tersely, in modern phraseology,
is simply "whiz without fizz!"*[38]

WILLIE TAKES COMMAND

William Bradley Daniels passed away on Christmas Eve in 1890. He
died aged sixty-five, after a period of declining health following a
carriage accident and a series of strokes that followed. The protracted
legal wrangling with his third wife likely also played a part in wearing
him down. He desired cremation, a highly unusual practice at the time, so
partner Fisher and estate executor Judge Mitchell Benedict accompanied
the body east to Detroit (then the closest crematory to Denver), where
it was cremated and the ashes divided. Half were placed in an urn and
buried beside the ashes of his second wife, Elizabeth, at Rosehill Cemetery
in Chicago. Newspaper accounts do not mention the division; this only
came to light much later (see chapter 7). William Cooke Daniels, then
twenty years old, was studying Buddhism in far off Yokohama, Japan,

when word of his father's passing reached him. Prior to his Japan trip, he had tried journalism, working a stint in New York as a cub reporter for the *New York Commercial Advertiser*. It was there that he became fast friends with another young journalist, Charles MacAllister Willcox, who would figure prominently in his, and the store's, futures.[39]

Willie Daniels had been a terror as a boy, setting fires to his schools on three separate occasions. As an only child, he was prone to tantrums, was doted on by the Mitchells and was subject to lung problems. His busy father didn't quite know what to do with him, so he sent him to school in Connecticut. He later dabbled in electrical engineering at the Boston Institute of Technology and spent a year at Yale before his New York newspapering phase. By the time he was a young man, "Will" (as he now preferred to be called) had developed the inquisitive mind and wanderlust that would mark his entire life. Despite his father's death, the young man did not immediately return to Denver; as a wealthy heir to a department store fortune, he would continue traveling, living six months on a yacht and two years in New Zealand, where he learned to fish and play polo.[40]

William Cooke Daniels, son of the founder and man of the world. *Ron and Judy Proctor collection.*

39

The fourth floor Tea Room, expanded and remodeled, circa 1907. *Denver Public Library, Western History Collection.*

William Garrett Fisher, although his name was on the door, was a junior partner, owning just one-third of Daniels and Fisher, while Daniels held two-thirds. With the senior Daniels frequently traveling and then dying when the junior was not yet of age, Fisher kept the store going strong though the tumultuous 1890s, adding a fifth floor in the dark year of 1893 (as mentioned in chapter 2), with full faith in the futures of Denver and Colorado. The new floor housed clothing manufacturing, freeing up space on lower floors to stock more merchandise than ever before. With approximately seven hundred employees, Daniels and Fisher was now the largest dry goods concern in the state and "perhaps the largest between Chicago and San Francisco."[41]

When, at twenty-seven, William Cooke Daniels finally returned to Denver, it was with the intention of becoming a businessman. After leaving New Zealand, he had visited various parts of the world, including two years (1895 through 1897) in Europe with his new wife, Edith Turner Daniels. Had Fisher not passed away during a business trip to New York in April 1897, he might have stayed there, but with both Fisher and his

William Cooke Daniels's remodeling made Daniels and Fisher the most elegant store in Denver. *Denver Public Library, Western History Collection.*

father gone, he had to return to Denver to settle things with Fisher's widow and take up his father's trade. He bought out Mrs. Fisher's interest, becoming sole owner of the store, and immediately set out to improve operations by incorporating innovations he had observed in other cities and other countries.[42]

Some of the changes were physical, such as remodeling the Sixteenth Street ground floor to finally acknowledge that it, and not the Lawrence Street side, was the store's primary façade. Daniels ordered the Sixteenth Street doors widened and had new bronze-framed show windows installed to capture pedestrians' attention. Inside, he spent thousands on elegant mahogany and beveled glass showcases and décor refinements. He moved the Tea Room to a larger space on the fourth floor. He introduced a book department, including out-of-town newspapers and national magazines, along with a bicycle shop to take advantage of the two-wheeler craze. In 1901, Daniels added a department selling jewelry, including custom creations. He installed a glass-enclosed floral shop chilled by one thousand pounds of ice delivered daily; customers could order flowers at Daniels and Fisher and have them sent to any address in the country, via telegraph to local florists. He expanded the store by buying more lots along Lawrence Street and building a new wing for the wholesale division, thus freeing up the fifth floor for additional retail space, including an elegant salon (the French Room) for custom dressmaking.[43]

Daniels also made operational changes, many of a kind that made him seem a latter-day version of Charles Dickens's paternalistic Fezziwig. Concerned that his young, school-age stock boys, cash boys and cash girls were missing their education by working long hours, he created an in-store school, housed in a room on the third floor. It operated six days each week, with classes segregated by age and a curriculum emphasizing arithmetic, spelling, composition and geography, initially taught by Denver North High School graduate Miss Ann Ecker. Employees were paid for time spent in class, an hour in the morning and another in the afternoon, and because they could be fired for misbehavior, discipline

Daniels installed elegant curving mahogany and glass display cases; this department sold handkerchiefs. *Denver Public Library, Western History Collection.*

The fifth-floor French Room was the destination for ladies seeking custom dresses. *Denver Public Library, Western History Collection.*

was never much of a problem. Of course, it could (and should) be argued that the children would have benefitted more by attending regular public or parochial school rather than working in a department store, but the Daniels and Fisher school was at least an effort to do right by its youngest staff members, a recognition that many children had to work to help support their families.[44]

Unusually for the period, Daniels and Fisher did not limit its hiring to people of white complexion, priding itself on its "liberal principles." It claimed that "a number of" its staff were African American, and it is therefore possible that others might have been Asian or Hispanic. Unknown is whether any of these non-Anglo staffers served customers on the sales floor or were restricted to behind-the-scenes duties.[45]

Under the younger Daniels, the store also instituted a new policy regarding business on summer Saturdays, the "Saturday Half-Holiday." Rather than stay open all afternoon during the warmer months from May to October, Daniels and Fisher closed at 1:00 p.m., allowing employees

The third-floor classroom for cash girls and boys. *Denver Public Library, Western History Collection.*

to spend their Saturday afternoons however they liked. Naturally, in that era before air conditioning, business was slow on summer Saturday afternoons, so the store's publicity department, in portraying the store as concerned for its workers, was also making the most of the cost-saving measure of not keeping people at their posts when store traffic was light. During the Christmas shopping season, Daniels instituted a policy of closing no later than 6:00 p.m. each day, so as not to overwork his clerks, a change that likely resulted in some lost evening transactions.[46]

Concerned about physical fitness, Daniels tried (but failed) to buy property near City Park for a ballpark so that employees could form baseball teams. He instituted paid vacations: any full-time employee with a year or more of service was eligible for two weeks of paid vacation time. Finally, in an early version of workers' compensation insurance, Daniels established an endowment fund with his own money (with employees also contributing) to provide for anyone who might not be able to work for extended periods of time due to accidents or illness. He credited this idea to Paris department store Bon Marché.[47]

Major Daniels

In 1898, a boiler blew up on the USS *Maine*, anchored in Havana harbor. Many of the crew members were killed, and America, perceiving it as a hostile act, went to war with Spain. Daniels was, like most men of his background and social class, intensely patriotic and immediately volunteered to serve in the army. As a wealthy merchant, he easily secured a commission as major. For the rest of his life, the Denver newspapers referred to him as "Major Daniels" in all accounts of his doings, possibly at his request, but also to flatter an advertiser. Serving under General Henry Lawton, Daniels saw action at the siege of Santiago, and the general later commended him for bravery under fire. Falling ill with typhoid fever, his military career soon ended, and he returned to Denver in 1899.[48]

Inspired by his war experiences, Daniels decided in 1902 that his young male employees would benefit from military training and so created the Daniels and Fisher Cadets. Wearing dark blue uniforms, the twenty-one boys, mostly fourteen or fifteen years old, drilled with real weapons on the store's roof and were said to handle them "like veterans." They marched

Major William Cooke Daniels (right) during the Spanish-American War, 1898. *History Colorado.*

The Daniels and Fisher Cadet Corps held practice on the store's roof. *Denver Public Library, Western History Collection.*

in parades and appeared at other public events. As a further expression of its owner's patriotism, in 1905, the store unfurled what it claimed was the world's largest American flag, measuring 115 feet across by 55 feet high and weighing 450 pounds. For the Grand Army Encampment, held in Denver that year, the store hung the flag from the cornice on the Sixteenth Street side. Stretching nearly the full width of the building (125 feet from Lawrence Street to the alley), it covered all of the windows on the third, fourth and fifth floors. In 1908, the store utilized even more red, white and blue when it won the contract to decorate Denver's new Municipal Auditorium for the Democratic National Convention, which nominated William Jennings Bryan for the presidency. The store's decorating department draped twenty thousand yards of bunting across the walls and ceiling of the hall and festooned all of the light poles on Fifteenth, Sixteenth and Seventeenth Streets, in enough fabric "to reach to Morrison."[49]

In 1898, Donna Madixxa's legal efforts to obtain a portion of her former husband's estate were finally exhausted. Lacking an heir, and perhaps

In 1905, the "World's Largest" American flag nearly obscured the Sixteenth Street façade. *Denver Public Library, Western History Collection.*

fearing that some future Lilyon (or Lilyon herself) might try the same thing again, Daniels decided in 1901 to incorporate the business as the Daniels and Fisher Stores Company. In addition to protecting his potential future heirs from a probate court, the new legal structure would allow him to bring in other partners and reward his most valued lieutenants. Officers of the new corporation included Daniels as president; the store's general manager, Charles MacAllister Willcox, as vice-president; and several others, including William D. Downs, who would later become a partner in Gano-Downs, a rival store several blocks up Sixteenth Street.[50]

Also in 1901, Major Daniels chartered the Daniels State Bank, which grew out of a proto-credit union run for the benefit of store employees. Its officers were mostly the same men as the new Stores Company, but also included in the group was a rising young banker, Alexis C. Foster. Initially quartered in the store, a year later, it moved two blocks up Sixteenth Street into a storefront, and in 1904, it was sold to Foster and other Denver businessmen (Daniels and Willcox retaining shares) and re-chartered as United States National Bank, with quarters in the Ernest and Cranmer Building at Seventeenth and Curtis Streets.[51]

General Manager Willcox was well known in Colorado by this time. After his arrival in Denver in 1890 (urged to come by Daniels when they were journalists together in New York), he worked as a reporter for the *Denver Times* and *Rocky Mountain News*. The son of Civil War general Orlando B. Willcox, he had been named as assistant adjutant general of Colorado in 1895, in which capacity he had commanded troops to fight the unions that had struck against the mine owners of Cripple Creek and Leadville. He had joined Daniels and Fisher in 1898, when Daniels had left for the Spanish-American War and needed both a trusted friend and someone with strong command skills to helm the store in his absence; it did not matter to Daniels that Willcox had no prior retail experience. In 1906, he married Marie DePazza Roberts of Independence, Missouri (he addressed letters to "my dearest Pazza"); in 1907, their daughter Elaine was born. In later years, Willcox would chair Mayor Robert W. Speer's Civic Center Commission, serve on Speer's Mountain Parks Board, serve on the Moffat Tunnel Commission, serve as treasurer for the Denver Press Club and serve as director on the boards of the Denver Art Museum and the United States National Bank.[52]

With these business changes having been made, Major Daniels felt comfortable enough with life and with Willcox that he left Denver again early in 1902, not to return for five years. He left Edith at home, and the couple quietly divorced (shortly thereafter she married someone else). Daniels's first stop was French Guiana in South America, prospecting for gold. Then he went on to nearby British Guinea, where he spent seven weeks being towed up a river in search of diamonds, "penetrating further into the interior of the country than any white man had," as avidly reported by the *Denver Post*.[53]

Sailing next for England, he chanced to stop at Martinique two days after the worst volcanic disaster of its time, the eruption of Mount Pelée, which had killed over thirty thousand people and destroyed the

Charles MacAllister Willcox ran Daniels and Fisher from 1898 until 1929. *Denver Public Library, Western History Collection.*

town of Saint-Pierre. Daniels took extensive photos of the aftereffects, which were reproduced in the Denver papers. In England, he connected with the Royal Geographical Society, which was planning an expedition to Papua New Guinea. Daniels dipped into his own pocket to help fund the expedition, and the society named it the "Daniels Ethnographical Expedition" in his honor. The group, which included Daniels, several scientists and a professional photographer, spent two years on the island studying its people and natural ecosystems, taking thousands of photos (many by Daniels) and collecting specimens and artifacts. After returning to Europe, Daniels went to Paris to help write up a two-volume report on the expedition's findings.[54]

Daniels returned to Denver finally in 1907, pleased with what he saw. Speaking to reporters, he was sunnily optimistic yet castigating, in Theodore Rooseveltian phraseology, those who said the state's prosperity was fragile: "Why, any Colorado man who admits himself a pessimist these days ought to be shot for his stupid folly and his bones put in a museum along with those of the other extinct species they dig out of the sand banks! Dead, he might amuse the paleontologists—but alive he'd be no god use to us nor to himself." He stayed in town just two months before disappearing again. In early April came the stunning news that he had voyaged to England to marry a Miss Cicely Banner, who, as the daughter of Caroline York Somers, could trace her ancestry back to King Edward I and was related to half the names in the *Illustrated London News*. Denver was wowed, and the papers were suddenly filled with the genealogies of British aristocrats—the Duke of Bedford, the Duchess of Somerset, Lord and Lady Hyde—that few in the city had contemplated previously. Daniels had first encountered her, all of twenty-two years of age, through her guardian, the Bishop of Rochester (in Kent), whom Daniels had met in Melbourne, Australia, after his New Guinea expedition.[55]

Taking a "country place near London," it would be two years before the married couple would make their first Denver appearance, accompanied by Cicely's dearest friend, Miss Florence Martin of New South Wales. The new Mrs. Daniels was an immediate hit with the press. The *Denver Post* described her as "vivacious, extremely fair to look upon and possess[ing] a personality of unusual charm." As a true daughter of the English upper crust, the paper continued, "She rides and drives and motors and is fond of pets and wears beautiful gowns and is in love with America and the American people." But in some ways, she was perhaps a bit too advanced for provincial Denver: "No one could object to Mrs. Daniels smoking a cigarette if they once saw her perform this feat, which to the average American is an act in itself which

Cicely Banner Daniels, circa 1909. *Ron and Judy Proctor collection.*

does not inspire a sentiment of admiration." However, smoking was a minor flaw, and it didn't matter anyway, as Cicely Daniels was not destined to join Denver's high society. After their visit, the major and his wife went back to Europe, leasing a fifteenth-century castle (Château de la Motte d'Usseau) near Tours, France, as well as a home in England, near Worcester.[56]

THE TOWER STORE

William Cooke Daniels, however, was not done with Denver, the source of his fortune, and in fact, what came next is what he's chiefly remembered for. Although he had contemplated expanding across the alley as early as 1900, it wasn't until February 1910 that exciting news came of an "artistic improvement" he planned to build. He had signed a lease with John Alkire, owner of the property at Sixteenth and Arapahoe Streets, and had further purchased the Merchant's Publishing Company quarters next to the Alkire Block on Arapahoe. Both buildings would shortly come down, and in their place, something very special would arise, a landmark indeed.

Once expanded across the alley, the new Daniels and Fisher store would run for 266 feet along Sixteenth Street, and patrons would enter via a new main entrance at the base of a tower on the Arapahoe corner. This monument, to become Denver's tallest building, would rise 330 feet from the sidewalk to the dome of the cupola, which would be topped by a flagpole, the Stars and Stripes fluttering 375 feet above the Denver plain. The Daniels and Fisher Tower, its design modeled on the Campanile of St. Mark's in Venice, would boast an observation deck "from which [could] be obtained an indescribably grand view of the most remarkable panorama of mountains and plains in the world." A massive clock, illuminated at night, would be visible on each of its four sides, providing the answer to "what time is it?" to anyone who asked for miles around. The old building would be remodeled to conform to the style of the new, Italian with a "strong Roman Palazzo feeling," sheathed in buff-colored tapestry brick and matte-finished terra cotta, capped with a red-tile roof. The Lawrence Street façade, now clearly secondary, would remain largely untouched, retaining its 1870s design. Above the first floor, which would be split by the alley running through the block, the two buildings would be joined as one. Altogether, the store would now spread across 400,475 square feet, or about nine acres. Designed by the prestigious firm of Frederick Junius Sterner and George Hebard Williamson (with Sterner the principle architect), the new building's aesthetic represented Daniels's desire to "get away from the inartistic 'warehouse' style of construction" of most department stores, which were "bald and ugly, utilitarian and unlovely." Most of the other leading stores, particularly the store's chief rival, Denver Dry Goods, were built of common red brick. Daniels and Fisher would show that a department store could be elegant in the European sense, a "triumph of the builder's art." [57]

In 1911, the expansion was nearly complete, with the Lawrence Street building still sporting its Victorian façade, soon to be remodeled. *Denver Public Library, Western History Collection.*

A skyscraper that would rival those of eastern metropolises meant that Denver had joined the ranks of America's big cities, an impressive feat for a town little more than five decades old. The store claimed it would rank as the third-tallest building in the country, after New York's Singer Sewing Machine Company and Metropolitan Life towers, although there were two

Observation deck visitors enjoyed this view up Sixteenth Street looking toward the Capitol. *Denver Public Library, Western History Collection.*

other buildings, one in New York and another in Philadelphia, that were more than 330 feet high in 1910 (making the D&F Tower the sixth-tallest). But this was no mere tall building: the Daniels and Fisher Tower was part of Denver's great transformation. The announcement came during the administration of Mayor Robert W. Speer, who since 1904 had worked to remake the city along more artistic, "City Beautiful" lines, with parkways, Municipal Auditorium, a proposed Civic Center and other projects. The Daniels and Fisher Tower was a privately built response to his public works.[58]

The tower was more than a civic ornament, however. As the tallest building in town, it also symbolized the commercial enterprise that built it. Confident in the tower's emblematic value, the store claimed it would not have need of any exterior signage in the manner of other stores, nor would it install the usual awnings to destroy the Italian Renaissance composition (neither claim proved true—tasteful bronze signs were installed, as were sun-deflecting awnings, crucial in that pre-air-conditioned time). The *Denver Times* called the tower "one of the best advertisements the institution ever enjoyed."[59]

The tower figured prominently in all advertising, including matches. *Ron and Judy Proctor collection.*

It would also be useful: each floor had a designated purpose. Female staff would use some for break rooms and lunchrooms (segregated by age, with cash girls not mingling with senior sales ladies). The fifteenth floor would house the school and another floor a "hospital," with a nurse on duty during business hours. The male buying staff would have a floor fitted out as a gentleman's club, with fine furnishings, a billiard table and the latest periodicals. Cash boys would have their floor, where they could relax and play games between shifts. The fourteenth floor, with its column-framed balconies, would serve as a dining room for store functions or it could be booked by anyone for special occasions. Charles MacAllister Willcox would occupy the twelfth floor. Above all, the twentieth floor would greet paying customers ascending by elevator and climbing stairs to emerge on the observation deck high above Sixteenth Street. After viewing distant sights through telescopes, they could buy a souvenir in the store's curio shop before

No tourist's itinerary would be complete without an elevator ride to the observation balcony. *Author's collection.*

descending to the street. By placing all of these functions in the tower, the store could devote maximum square footage on the main five floors and basement to retail use.[60]

The tower was, until the First National Bank tower at Seventeenth and Welton Streets overtook it in 1958, the tallest element in Denver's skyline, equally visible from open prairie outside of town and windows of passenger trains pulling into Union Station. In fact, it symbolized Denver more than any other building. In loving tribute, architect Alan Fisher (no relation to William Garrett Fisher) wrote decades later:

> *It was the first building that you'd see when you came to Denver, Colorado, on the Burlington Route or the Union and Pacific Railroad Line. You'd see it first on Christmas Holidays home from school; you'd see it first from about old Riverside Cemetery at the cottonwood bend of the Platte. You'd see it from the vestibule of the olivegreen Pullman car as it roared by the quiet cemetery where great Governor Evans was in repose; where your own grandmother was sleeping under winter leafless trees, now all in afternoon sun; and Augusta Tabor there, too, still indignant in death over her plight in life...Daniels and Fisher Tower would be the first you'd see and you'd be home again where you belonged and where you wanted to be and where your fathers had come long ago...and where, if luck held out, you would probably stay and add your part and be in respect of the things that had been done there long before for you.[61]*

Why did Daniels choose the Campanile of St. Mark's as the model for his tower? Why did he not, given his anglophile tendencies and English wife, base it on the clock tower ("Big Ben") at the Houses of Parliament in London or on any other distinctive European tower? It might just have been that Daniels was following a trend.[62] The original Campanile of St. Mark's—built during the Middle Ages, completed in the twelfth century and significantly rebuilt in the sixteenth—had suddenly collapsed into a pile of bricks on July 14, 1902. Over the following decade, the Euro-American world's attention was focused on Venice's rebuilding effort, which sparked a vogue for replicas in cities all over the world. In addition to the Daniels and Fisher Tower, others inspired by St. Mark's built in the decades following the Venice collapse include those of King Street Station in Seattle; North Station in Toronto; Brisbane, Australia's city hall; Sather Tower at the University of California–Berkeley and others. In New York City, two replicas were built on a larger scale: Bankers Trust Company at 14 Wall Street and the Metropolitan Life Insurance Company on Madison Square. The Daniels and Fisher Tower would open six months after its Venetian counterpart was re-dedicated, but as the always boastful local press was fond of pointing out, while both buildings had forty-foot-square footprints, Denver's tower was one foot taller than Venice's.[63]

Demolition of the Alkire and Merchant's Publishing buildings began in May 1910, simultaneous with the release of an architectural rendering published in all four Denver daily papers. An artistic covered wooden arcade soon went up around the site, designed with arched openings like the building that would soon arise behind it, with construction offices housed in a cupola-topped building elevated over the corner of Sixteenth and Arapahoe Streets. Excavation—the deepest hole yet seen in Denver for construction of a building—soon commenced, and by late summer the foundation had been laid. The steel-framed tower had its own foundation, separate from that of the rest of the building, a single block of concrete teen feet thick that was meant to support twenty thousand tons (the weight of the occupied tower plus the force of high winds on it). Construction was swift, aided by night work illuminated by electric floodlights. By December 30, the steelworkers were able to hoist an American flag more than three hundred feet above the sidewalk for their topping-out ceremony.[64]

A *Denver Post* photographer attended this windy ritual. Not being used to great heights, he was in awe of the view and the sensation of being so high in the sky (with no solid walls surrounding him): "Far below was Sixteenth street, and though it was teeming with life, not a sound reached us high up in the skies. The cars looked like the mechanical electric toys that are displayed in the holiday dressed windows of the stores, while the people looked as if they were Lilliputs." Denver seen from above was now the "Dream City."[65]

The parade of superlatives continued, as the store took advantage of publicity on numerous occasions during 1911 to build excitement for the completion and opening. In March, the tower's bell arrived, described (perhaps accurately, perhaps not) as "the largest bell west of the Mississippi," six feet high and weighing 5,500 pounds. Arriving at Union Station from a Baltimore foundry, the bell was paraded up Sixteenth Street to the *Denver Post* at 1544 Champa Street and then paraded back down to Arapahoe for hoisting into the tower, while "thousands along the sidewalks looked on with admiration." In July, *Electrical World* magazine paid the city a visit. Every downtown property owner was asked to turn on all of the lights in his building, and citizens were urged to flood the streets with humanity as magazine photographers took pictures from the tower for nationwide distribution, advertising Denver as the "City of Lights." A carnival atmosphere prevailed, with the *Denver Post* Boys' Band marching down Sixteenth Street to the beat of a drum played by Carl Sandell, "the biggest drum major in the world." The seven-foot, five-inch (sometimes listed as seven foot four or seven foot three) Sandell, after leaving the band, would become a living symbol of Daniels and Fisher, serving as the store's doorman outside the Tower entrance for five decades. He represented the store in parades, opened doors for the famous (John D. Rockefeller Jr., Henry Ford) and was so well known that he was even considered for the role of Goliath in the Twentieth Century Fox biblical epic *David and Bathsheba*.[66]

Curiously, despite Willcox's and Daniels's canny mastery of publicity, the store did not have a formal grand opening when all was finished. It opened the new wing in stages beginning in spring, as soon as the plasterers and painters were done, letting shoppers get used to the new,

Towering Carl Sandell served as Daniels and Fisher doorman from 1911 until the store closed in 1958. *Denver Public Library, Western History Collection.*

spacious layout gradually. "We do not care for formal openings," the store's advertising manager told the *Times*, "preferring to let our merchandise and treatment of patrons speak for us." Regardless, during the first week of November, when all sections were complete and open and the old building joined with the new, management filled the store with a blaze of white, celebratory chrysanthemums. Thousands of curious shoppers soon filled every aisle on every floor. The newly expanded and remodeled store, and

The tower's silhouette looms over this 1920s Sixteenth Street winter scene. *Author's collection.*

the tower in particular, quickly became a point of pride for Denverites. It was the most talked-about building in town, eclipsing all others in prestige, and no tourist's itinerary would be complete without a visit.[67]

The new building also allowed the store more dining amenities. The Tea Room moved to the fourth floor of the new Arapahoe building. Seating 450, its décor featured murals of Venetian scenes painted by Tim Carson, and the room could be booked by organizations for meetings after store hours. On the first floor, a shopper could grab a bite at the Fountain Room; elsewhere in the building, an employee cafeteria sold meals at cost. The fourteenth-floor dining room (mentioned above) was christened the "Blue Room," for the predominant paint color, perhaps inspired by the blue in the Della Robbia medallions on the building's exterior.[68]

The Denver press, as well as publicity seekers, quickly grasped the tower's symbolic power. On election night in May, 1912, the *Denver Republican*, whose offices were directly across Sixteenth Street from the store, projected stereopticon slides on a large white sheet on the building's façade and installed a beacon at the very top, under the cupola's dome, using six thousand watts of incandescent tungsten bulbs to flash election returns across miles of dark sky. In order to understand the meaning of the flashes, one had to have previously purchased a copy of that morning's *Republican* (whether or not it was effective, the paper never repeated the stunt). In 1918, Jack Williams, the "Human Fly," climbed the tower, from sidewalk to the dome, as a publicity stunt to raise money for U.S. Marines recruitment. Of course, the tower also inevitably became a focus for the suicidal, with some achieving oblivion and others just gravely injuring themselves.[69]

THE GRIM YEAR: 1918

William Cooke Daniels, after directing the tower's design and construction from his homes in Europe, visited Denver just once after the expansion was complete, in 1912. When World War I broke out two years later, he was ready to get back into the fight. Once the United States entered the war in 1917, he volunteered his services but was rejected due to physical disabilities related to the typhoid he had suffered during his earlier military adventure in Cuba and expedition in New Guinea. He continued to travel during the war, perhaps in connection with some sort of non-military service to the government (the Denver papers hinted it

Florence Martin's gift to Denver, Daniels Park, features this rustic picnic pavilion, designed by Jules Jacques Benoit Benedict. From *Denver Municipal Facts.*

was likely). In 1918, his dreams ended. He went to Buenos Aires, where he was a guest of Frederick Watts, an old friend. He contracted a serious fever and died on the eighteenth of March; he was just forty-seven years old. Like his father, he was cremated.[70]

Cicely Daniels, who remained in Europe with Florence Martin while her husband traveled, followed him to the grave in October of that same grim year. She and Martin had been spending the war in neutral Switzerland, where Major Daniels had sent them for their safety. The women ran a club for recuperating soldiers, teaching the men rug weaving. Running out of wool, they traveled to England to buy more and checked into Claridge's, London's fashionable hotel. Both soon fell ill with influenza—the entire world was in the midst of a pandemic. Florence Martin survived, but Cicely Daniels succumbed.[71]

William Cooke Daniels and Cicely Banner Daniels left sizeable estates, but lacking an heir, ownership of the store passed out of the founding family. A majority share went to Daniels and Fisher Stores Company president Charles MacAllister Willcox and to his daughter, Elaine Willcox, an eleven-year-old girl. Ever eager to please one of its largest advertisers, the *Post* described young Elaine Willcox as "a winsome, charming little miss of an exceptionally bright mind." Among Denver observers, it was generally felt that the Danielses' wills had left the store to the Willcoxes not only as a mark of their friendship but also to keep it in the hands of Denver people. As cosmopolitan and worldly as William Cooke Daniels was, he had a great fondness for the provincial city, and he had always believed in its possibilities.[72]

A minority ownership share went to Florence Martin. She eventually came to Denver to look after her new interests and ended up staying for the rest of her long life. The Denver Mountain Parks system benefitted from her largesse when she donated 1,040 acres twenty-one miles south of Denver in rural Douglas County to create a memorial to her friends. Located between Castle Rock and today's suburb of Highlands Ranch, thousands of visitors annually enjoy Daniels Park, with its expansive views of the South Platte River Valley.[73]

Chapter 5
AGING GRACEFULLY

Daniels and Fisher is an old store in point of time. It is vital, alert, alive, youthful in point of view, employing the wisdom and knowledge gained from experience and leadership, but developing its program to meet the requirements of a rushing, lavish, practical, luxurious age.[74]

A DENVER STORE OWNED BY DENVER PEOPLE

Under the ownership of Charles MacAllister Willcox; his daughter, Elaine; and Florence Martin, Daniels and Fisher continued to thrive. Willcox constantly looked for ways to improve the store (for instance, in 1922, he installed a soda fountain with ice cream–making machinery) and retain its status as Denver's leading store. While it had long contended in the department store trade with Denver Dry Goods, May Company and Joslin's, by the 1920s, there was a new level of intensity, fueled by that decade's easy money. Although they were not full-line department stores, Daniels and Fisher competed for the carriage trade with Gano-Downs, A.T. Lewis and Son and Neusteter's, clustered several blocks up Sixteenth at Stout Street. In the 1910s and 1920s, all three had embarked on ambitious expansions that drew attention and customers away from reliable Daniels and Fisher. While these latter three could boast Denver ownership, Denver Dry Goods, May and Joslin's could not, being controlled by corporations

Above: A Jazz Age hatbox featuring a stylized tower. *Robert and Kristen Autobee collection.*

Left: Daniels and Fisher courted the carriage trade, evident from this 1923 theater program advertisement. *Author's collection.*

based elsewhere. The store's advertising department during the Willcox years and later made sure to remind shoppers that Daniels and Fisher was still owned by Denver people.[75]

A CAREER WOMAN

In 1927, Mary Alice Fitzgerald, who would become a Denver bookselling legend, joined the staff. A New York City native, she had come to Denver in 1919 as a nineteen-year-old hoping to cure her tuberculosis in Colorado's dry climate. She spent four years living in the Oakes Home, a higher-class sanitarium on West Thirty-second Avenue and Decatur Street. It took several years, but she was eventually able to lead a relatively normal life, leasing an apartment, making friends and shopping for books, one of her passions. Her mother, who lived with her, was very much against the idea of her working, worried that the tuberculosis could recur. One day, after seeing a friend off at Union Station, she stopped by Daniels and Fisher and found herself in the book department, which occupied the third-floor alley bridge between the two buildings. She had a long conversation with the department manager, who told Fitzgerald she was looking for temporary help during the Christmas season and asked if

A circa 1947 book signing. *From left*: unidentified, store president Edward C. Yourell, book buyer Mary Alice Fitzgerald, author Virginia Sorensen (sitting) and store advertising manager Margaret Harvey. *Denver Public Library, Western History Collection.*

she'd be interested. Mary accepted immediately (facing the music with her mother when she got home that day but prevailing), and when the buyer resigned after Christmas, she recommended Mary take over her position. Mary rode the elevator to Willcox's twelfth-floor office for an interview and was immediately impressed with the collection of rare books he kept there and told him so. For his part, he decided immediately that "she really knew books" and offered her the position.[76]

Daniels and Fisher's book department was not large, but it had character and a well-selected inventory that included literary classics, cooking and art; about one-third of the space was devoted to children's books. The stock was displayed on antique tables and in "old Victorian cabinets running from floor to ceiling." Over-stuffed chairs allowed browsers to sit for a while to decide whether they wanted to buy a book. In an oral history Fitzgerald gave in 1997, the interviewer made a comparison to a more recent bookstore: "It sounds like the way the Tattered Cover is now." Fitzgerald responded affirmatively, and when the interviewer said she thought that was a "totally new idea," Fitzgerald countered with, "Nooo. That's the way that shop was."

Fitzgerald went on New York buying trips four times annually; her salary was not large, but as was true for all store buyers, her travel perks were good—first-class train accommodation, better hotels and a generous *per diem*. Once she was even sent to London to buy fine bindings. She personally served the store's better-known customers, including Ethel Merman Six (the Broadway diva was briefly married in the 1950s to Robert F. Six, an executive with then–Denver based Continental Airlines), First Lady Mamie Doud Eisenhower (she and Ike vacationed annually in Denver, where she had grown up) and *Denver Post* heiress May Bonfils. She had close relationships with Denver authors, who referred to her as "Mary Fitz." She hosted book signings for Thomas Hornsby Ferril (later Colorado's poet laureate), Marian Castle, Bill Barrett and the city's best-known literary celebrity of the day, playwright Mary Coyle Chase (*Harvey*). These were truly *social* events, with invitations sent out to the store's best customers, and were well attended. Her most thrilling interaction with fame came in 1951, when she won a national contest conducted by publisher G.P. Putnam's Sons, for selling the most copies of its big fall title, *A King's Story*. She was flown to New York, where she dined with the book's author, the Duke of Windsor, and his wife, the Duchess (formerly known as King Edward VIII of England and Mrs. Wallis Simpson).

TROTT, BEANS AND YOURELL

By 1929, Willcox felt it was time to retire after thirty-three years running the store. He and his daughter (now Princess Elaine Wilhelmine Willcox Odescalchi, having married a Hungarian prince), sold their shares to a new Denver-based investor group led by Alfred Blake Trott (most often referred to as "A.B.," probably a personal preference) and Walter Beans, both of whom had also been associated with the store for many years. Trott, who had worked at Daniels and Fisher since 1898, was the new president and Beans the treasurer. As before, the sellers' idea was to keep the institution in the hands of Denver people, and when they announced the $3 million sale to the press, they hinted that they had been offered even more by "Eastern syndicates."[77]

They were vague on this point, but in fact they had been offered money by easterners, and Willcox had seriously considered the offer. In 1928, Eugene Greenhut, an agent of Hahn Department Stores, Inc., spent some months in negotiation with Willcox's brother Orlando B. Willcox, a New York attorney who was also a Daniels and Fisher board member. Finally, in late February or early March 1929, Charles Willcox decided against Hahn, which had only formed the previous December as a holding company for twenty-two formerly independent department stores. It was fortuitous for Daniels and Fisher that he did so, as the financially stretched Hahn was forced to reorganize in 1935 (after bankruptcy, it was known as Allied Stores Corporation).[78] It may have been sentiment that led Willcox to this decision to keep Daniels and Fisher local, or it may have been money: the best offer made by Hahn was probably only in the neighborhood of $2.5 to $2.7 million, rather than the $3 million paid by Trott and Beans. Charles MacAllister Willcox lived only three years after selling the store he had managed and owned for so many years, succumbing to pneumonia on October 19, 1932.[79]

The new owners' biggest physical change was the 1930 addition of a 450-car parking structure to the Arapahoe Street side of the building (this would be the final addition to the store, fifty-five years after Daniels and Fisher had first occupied the Sixteenth and Lawrence corner). In the William Cooke Daniels tradition, it was not utilitarian in design; the architects were careful to match the Italian Renaissance style and materials first used in the 1911 addition. This was quite an innovation, allowing for the first time the ability to park one's car in a spot that was guaranteed to be close to the store and enter it directly from the garage without ever being exposed to inclement weather (the store provided valet service, as a matter of course). It was also the first dedicated parking structure attached to any department store in Denver, meant to give it an edge against the competition—no other store could boast its own enclosed parking for quite some time. The next store that would have its own garage would be May-D&F, but that's getting ahead of the story.[80]

Solving Shoppers' Parking Problem

The new $200,000 garage and floral shop of the Daniels & Fisher Stores Co., which will be formally opened tomorrow. Top: An exterior view of the new addition, showing the electrically-operated Italian cut doors. Bottom: An interior view showing the Italian tiled floors. Mrs. Olivia Collins is alighting from her motor.

Daniels and Fisher's 1930 parking garage, a first for a Denver store.
Denver Public Library, Western History Collection.

Santa Claus beckons shoppers in this 1930s view from the roof of rival Joslin's. *Thomas J. Noel collection.*

Due To Ice Shortage We Are Unable To Serve Iced Tea or Coffee

APPETIZERS AND SOUPS

Grapefruit Juice, Orange Juice or V-8 Cocktail 15
Beef Bouillon . . . . cup 15   bowl 20
Vegetable Soup . . . . cup 15   bowl 20
Chicken Broth with Rice . . . . cup 15   bowl 20

SANDWICHES

American Cheese Sandwich 25
Peanut Butter and Jelly Sandwich 20
Ham Salad 20
Ripe Olive and Nut 35
Colonial Club Sandwich—Sliced Tongue, Chicken and Tomato 60
D. & F. Club Sandwich 65
Bacon and Tomato with Lettuce and Mayonnaise 40
Sliced Chicken with Lettuce and Mayonnaise 55
Baked Virginia Ham Sandwich 35

SALADS AND SALAD COMBINATIONS

Combination Fresh Vegetable Salad 45
Old-fashioned Fruit Salad with Egg & Relish Sandwich on Toast 55
Sliced Tomatoes 30
Fresh Fruit Plate with Cottage Cheese 75

BEVERAGES

Coffee, per cup 10, per pot 15   Postum per pot 15
Tea, per pot 10   Chocolate per cup 15
Individual Bottle of Milk or Buttermilk 10
Chocolate Milk 10
Glass of Half and Half 25

*Extra on Luncheon
Service not less than 25c
(Extra Charge for Single Portion Served Two Persons)
All prices are our ceiling prices, or below. By O. P. A.
regulations our ceilings are based on our highest
prices from April 4 to April 10, 1943.

TODAY'S SUGGESTIONS

Served with Rolls, Dessert, Coffee, Tea or Milk.

Creamed Mushrooms and Sweet Breads on Toast
with Mashed Potatoes and Peas 65
Browned Beef Hash with Spanish Cole Slaw 55
Tomato Aspic Salad and Cottage Cheese 65
Steamed Finnan Haddie with Parsley Potato & Green Beans 65
Fresh Shrimp Salad with Sliced Tomato 85
Chicken Patty with Sweet Potato & Peas 75
Fresh Garden Vegetable Plate 60
Roast Spring Chicken with Dressing
Mashed Potatoes and Peas 1.00

A LA CARTE SPECIALS

Served with Hot Rolls and Coffee, Tea or Milk.

Eggs Fried, Scrambled, Poached or Plain Omelette
with Bacon & Browned Potatoes 50

DESSERTS

Ginger Bread with Whipped Cream 15
Iced Watermelon or Canteloupe 15
Apricot Short Cake 25
Sherbet or Ice Cream and Sherbet 15
French-Apple or Custard Pie 15
Shadow Layer Cake 15
Cup Custard with Caramel Sauce 15
Royal Plums or Figs 15

Monday, September 10, 1945

A Tea Room menu from 1945 reflects wartime restrictions. *Ron and Judy Proctor collection.*

Daniels and Fisher survived the Great Depression in fine style; by 1939, Trott could declare a profit of $5.27 per share, up from $4.83 per share a year earlier. Trott died in 1944 (another record year, $8.32 profit per share), and Beans succeeded him for a short period. In 1946, with World War II over and stores all over downtown announcing expansion and remodeling plans to satisfy pent-up consumer demand, Edward C. Yourell succeeded Beans, who retired. Within a year, the new president announced a $2 million remodeling plan, including six new elevators, the store's first escalator (connecting just the first and second floors) and a $75,000 beauty salon complete with a soundproof room for facials.[81]

THE DOWAGER OF SIXTEENTH STREET

Not everything was a change for the better. There were ominous signs that the store was not in the best location anymore. In earlier years, Sixteenth and Lawrence was, in commercial real estate terms, the "100 percent corner," the epicenter of the city's retail trade, with Daniels and Fisher, May Company and Golden Eagle (Leopold Guldman's discount department store) occupying three of the four corners. Now, the 100 percent corner was either at Sixteenth and Stout (Gano-Downs, Neusteter's and variety store W.T. Grant, occupying the former A.T. Lewis space) or a block southeast, at California (Denver Dry Goods and after 1952, a six-story J.C. Penney). A block down Sixteenth from Daniels and Fisher, Larimer Street had become the heart of Denver's skid row over the previous decades, and blight was rapidly spreading across lower downtown. After Golden Eagle went out of business at the onset of World War II, it was not replaced by another department store that could generate similar traffic but instead by a western wear store and a cheap "credit store"; May Company had relocated farther uptown as early as 1906. Daniels and Fisher was isolated, so it was not too shocking when in 1948 the store experienced a robbery during business hours. Douglas Aylesworth, described as a "has-been Hollywood bit-part actor" posing as an armored car driver, absconded with $30,000 in cash and checks. Despite the beloved landmark tower, still visible from everywhere, the store felt remote from better parts of downtown. Located so far from the center, profits began to decline from their wartime highs.[82]

The store might be fading, but it was still elegant:

> *I remember going into the old D&F store…it was considered the most elegant of all the department stores, very sedate inside, with lots of solid wood trim on the main floor interior, where women stood behind wooden and glass display cases, spaced two to a counter, all around the peripheral wall. There, you could see the most exquisite little dainty linen and lace handkerchiefs, only by request. The white gloved women were there to pull it out for you to see more closely, but you weren't allowed to touch the hanky until you bought it.*[83]

The 1950s began with good news for the store: for the first time since the nineteenth century, when it had had a branch in Leadville, Daniels and Fisher was expanding within Colorado by buying the Giddings Company, a downtown Colorado Springs department store at Tejon and Kiowa Streets. Eventually, the Daniels and Fisher name went up on the Giddings building, and the store opened a branch in that city's Broadmoor Hotel. This was a logical move during an era of corporate expansion and very western in character: an old Colorado firm buying another one. But Daniels and Fisher would soon lose its status as a Colorado institution entirely.[84]

On Sunday, July 19, 1953, the front page of the *Rocky Mountain News* carried the shouting headline "Zeckendorf Buys Big Block of D&F Stock." This was in much larger type than the front page's other headline announcing the armistice that ended the Korean War, showing just how big this news was to Denver readers. Developer William Zeckendorf had been trying unsuccessfully for eight years to get a project called Courthouse Square off the ground, several blocks up Sixteenth Street (between Tremont Street and Court Place), and he needed a department store to anchor it. Unable to persuade any store to sign a lease (he had previously tried snagging Denver Dry Goods, May Company, and Daniels and Fisher), he raised $1.6 million in New York and bought control of the store. (The full story of Zeckendorf's impact on Denver and its retailers is told in chapter 7.)[85]

Zeckendorf did not want to own a department store—he just needed one for his project. Chronically short of cash, he also needed to pay back his creditors and so retained control for less than a year, selling his interest in May 1954 to a partnership composed of Younker Brothers department store of Des Moines, Iowa, and Jerome M. Ney of Fort Smith, Arkansas, who controlled a number of other Midwestern stores. Before he sold the business, he made sure he had his tenant: Daniels and Fisher president Albert P. Sonneman (who had replaced Yourell in 1951) had signed the lease to move uptown to Courthouse Square, once it was built, although as of 1954, there was no definitive completion date. Zeckendorf chose Younkers and Ney over several other better-known retail names that might have tried to get out of the lease; he felt safer with the Midwesterners.[86]

Meanwhile, sales continued to deteriorate at the old Tower Store, dropping from $9.4 million in 1952 to just under $9 million in 1953. Something had to be done to keep the store viable until it could make its move, and the new owners set their sights high, proclaiming that Daniels and Fisher had "the potential of becoming one of the great department stores in this country, because of the high esteem in which it is rightfully held throughout the entire West." Needing a visionary who could make that happen, they found Joseph Ross, who had begun his career at Macy's and was then a ten-year veteran of that storied Dallas institution, Neiman-Marcus (his career there took him from assisting store president Stanley Marcus to vice-president of merchandising). As the new president, the forty-year-old Ross quickly recognized that Daniels and Fisher had become dowdy and needed updating; he told the press he hoped to "set the town on its ear." He wanted "the nation to think in terms of D&F when it thinks of Denver as it thinks of Marshall Field's when Chicago is mentioned."[87]

To "re-establish the store's greatness," Ross promoted three principles: that Daniels and Fisher should "preserve the psychology of a small store," to make each customer feel special; to create "character" in the store, so that customers can decide "whether it is imaginative and progressive, whether it is a gracious host, what kind of home it has"; and to recognize the importance of esthetics" because "the day of strictly utilitarian merchandising is over."

He swiftly set about improving the quality of the store's incoming stock and drastically marked down years of accumulated, dated merchandise to purge it from inventory. He redecorated, even though the store would not be in its old home long, because "we have no intention of getting off a sick bed and hobbling on crutches into our new store." He commissioned an elegant new logo, one that would still look fresh today, and he overhauled the store's entire graphic look to go along with it, with new bags, more white space and lighter fonts in the advertising and other hallmarks of a more upscale store. He increased the number of buyers' trips, he established a department devoted to staging fashion shows, and he established "de luxe gift wrapping for all holidays," an idea he borrowed from his mentor, Stanley Marcus. Behind the scenes, he created an employee stock ownership plan to reward loyalty and excellent service.[88]

"The minute he came into the store, things started to buzz," Virginia York, the store's telephone operator, told the *Post*. Decades later, fondly remembering this exciting period, Mary Alice Fitzgerald told an interviewer that "in his first five minutes there he shook some dust out of that musty old store. Buyers were terrified they would lose their jobs, and a few did,

This mid-1950s Christmas catalogue shows Joe Ross's influence, with elegant graphics and giftwrapping designs (left). Inside (right), Ross catered to young baby boomers with locally produced western wear and popular Disney merchandise. *Denver Public Library, Western History Collection.*

Daniels and Fisher's environs showed signs of decline in 1956. *Denver Public Library, Western History Collection.*

but mostly Joe Ross was a kind man who wanted to inspire everyone to get the store moving again…he was Mr. Show Biz and he had vision." For his part, Ross greatly admired Fitzgerald, looking to her as the "official hostess for the whole store" and as "his sounding board for ideas." Ross created an art gallery adjacent to her book department and gave it to Fitzgerald to run. Artist Vance Kirkland was among the jurors for a November 1955 exhibition of Colorado artists, which featured work by Herbert Bayer, among others.[89]

Ross's energies (he was known to work long hours) paid off: by the end of the first fiscal year under his leadership, the store reported sales growth of $1.2 million over the prior year, an increase of over 14 percent. Sadly, the Ross era was not a long one, and Denver never got the chance to see the wonders he could accomplish with the new store at Courthouse Square: William Zeckendorf was not finished with Daniels and Fisher.[90]

Part II

WATCH US GROW

Chapter 6
ANOTHER PIONEER MERCHANT

Competitors Overwhelmed With Defeat!
Prices Split to Splinters!
Red-Handed Carnage!
We've Ground Prices to Powder![91]

BLUE JEANS AND BALL GOWNS

Before completing the Daniels and Fisher story, we must return to an earlier time. In 1877, Leadville, Colorado, where Daniels and Fisher would soon go into partnership with Smith, saw the birth of a retail empire that would endure until 2005. May Company, originally engaged in selling work clothes and supplies to miners, grew to become the largest department store chain in the United States. From its earliest days, May's motto was "Watch Us Grow." Colorado, and then the rest of the nation, did just that.

May Company founder David ("Dave" to friends) T. May was born in 1848 in Kaiserslautern, in the Rhine Palatinate in Bavaria. His shopkeeper father, struggling financially, decided when David was fifteen that he should migrate to the United States, where relatives had gone previously, to make his way. He landed in New York in 1863, and after a trip to Cincinnati paid for by an uncle living there, he soon found himself employed by a dry goods shop in Hartford City, Indiana, owned by a man named Kirschbaum.

He was an energetic and ambitious salesman, helping triple the business in just his first two years there, and soon became junior partner.[92]

One winter night in early 1877, a nearby building caught fire, its flames threatening the Kirschbaum & May store. May spent the entire night saving the stock, carrying merchandise to safety, ignoring the drenching he was receiving from fire hoses and snow on a freezing night. Shortly afterward, he developed pneumonia, which threatened to turn into tuberculosis. On doctor's orders to spend time in a dryer climate, May decided to leave Indiana. He sold his share of the shop for $25,000 and headed to Colorado. Arriving in the resort town of Manitou Springs, he was soon invited to join a fishing party at Twin Lakes, in the Arkansas River Valley south of Leadville. The party included Chicago department store magnate Marshall Field, along with other well-heeled men. Arriving at Twin Lakes, they heard stories of the riches to be found at nearby Leadville and decided to investigate.[93]

Pioneer merchant David May. *Missouri History Museum.*

Getting rich through unscientific prospecting is usually impossible, but the always-optimistic May tried, joining up with another greenhorn, Jake Holcomb. They dug holes for some weeks but had no luck. May knew retail, so he proposed to Holcomb that they give up mining and enter into business together. Finding a storekeeper who wanted to sell out, they bought up his goods and opened May, Holcomb and Dean (there was a third partner for a short period). Their stock in trade was mostly red woolen underwear and blue denim "California Riveted Duck Clothing" made by Levi Strauss and Company. In future histories, the company always claimed that its first success came with "Levis and longies." Their "store" was not much more than a tent, essentially a wood-frame shack with a canvas roof. When May wanted to move into a permanent building, the other two men weren't willing to risk the cost and wanted out. After the partnership dissolved, May called his new sole proprietorship store at 318 Harrison Avenue the "Great Western Auction House and Clothing

Store." He gave Holcomb a job as bookkeeper; Holcomb continued working for May until 1925.

Leadville was booming, and May was a canny retailer. Knowing the town was flush with cash, he famously capitalized on the distress of a Chicago store that had bought far more expensive ball gowns than it could reasonably dispose of, even in such a large city. May made a bargain with this unnamed retailer and had the fancy velvet and brocade dresses shipped to Leadville. The town's women (those with money) snapped up the entire shipment, even at prices that ranged from $200 to $400.

May had competitors in Leadville, among them Joseph and Louis Shoenberg. Their brother Moses shortly became May's partner, with the store renamed "May and Shoenberg." In 1879, the year Daniels, Fisher and Smith opened in Leadville, Rosa Shoenberg joined her brothers in the two-mile-high city, and May soon fell in love with her; they married in 1880. That same year, the first May and Shoenberg branch opened in Pueblo. Other (short-lived) branches followed in various Colorado boomtowns, including Irwin (near Gunnison), Glenwood Springs and Aspen. Except for the Pueblo branch, these were operated under the May name alone—his brother-in-law was not a partner. In those early days, May took his business to any spot that seemed likely to make his fortune—a pattern that would continue.

May stayed in Leadville for several years, becoming a prominent member of the Temple Israel congregation, and his first two sons, Morton J. and Thomas, were born in Leadville. Lake County elected him treasurer for two two-year terms beginning in 1881, a successful Republican in a largely Democratic county. But boomtowns eventually go bust, and May sensed better opportunities elsewhere. May and Shoenberg dissolved their partnership in 1885 after Moses sold May his share and moved to Kansas City.

In 1888, May came to Denver on business and noticed that the Dreyfus Company, a shop in the Clayton Block (today known as the Granite Building) at Fifteenth and Larimer Streets, was going out of business. May, seizing an opportunity to make a lot of money quickly, bought out the distressed merchant for $31,000. He hired a brass band to play in front of the store, to grab attention, and slashed prices. Within a week the merchandise was gone, and May had embarked on another new path.

AN EMPIRE IN THE MAKING

May returned to Leadville to hold a closeout sale, and once that was done, he came back to Denver. In 1889, he leased a space at 1614 Larimer Street and opened the May Shoe & Clothing Company. Louis Shoenberg joined him, and together they took on all comers, competing fiercely with established retailers, including Daniels and Fisher. They adopted a pugnacious attitude, as reflected in over-the-top newspaper advertisements:

> *WHY WE REJOICE!*
> *It is with a feeling of triumph that we today recall the scenes in the Clothing Arena of Denver of but three years ago, previous to our arrival, when the merciless Clothing Gladiators were feasting at the expense of the masses, asking war-time prices for worthless plunder, holding high carnival over their ill-gotten gains, and compare them with the conditions of today.*
>
> *As Sheridan, dashing into Winchester, brought victory for his soldiers, so did THE MAY dash into the competitors' camp with victory for the toilers of the Silver State and open the flood gates of Eastern prices and Metropolitan styles to Western consumers.*
>
> *We now proudly unfurl our banner, upon which it is written: Cash, Pluck and Enterprise, the life-blood which flows freely in to the heart of our grand business.*[94]

Success came quickly, and May soon took over adjoining storefronts up to 1622 Larimer and later leased a Lawrence-facing storefront that he connected to the main shop by a bridge across the alley. Another competitor was Skinner Brothers & Wright, which occupied a prime corner spot at Sixteenth and Lawrence, opposite Daniels and Fisher. In 1895, May Company bought out the Skinner store and connected its premises to its other spaces. Then May bought the adjacent Brunswick Hotel on Sixteenth and joined it to the Skinner building, remodeling the combined structure with large plate-glass windows.

All of this expansion would have been impressive enough, but by the time of the Skinner Brothers purchase, May and his brothers-in-law had already embarked on something much bigger. In 1892, the men pooled their cash, taking advantage of an opportunity to buy a St. Louis department store, the Famous. It was only the seventh-ranked store in that city by volume but could be had for $150,000; May Company was now a chain with two links. (In 1911, May bought a St. Louis competitor, William Barr Dry Goods;

May Company's Lawrence Street store (1895–1906), opposite Daniels and Fisher. *Denver Public Library, Western History Collection.*

Baby shoes (circa 1898) given by May Company to young mothers. *Denver Public Library, Western History Collection.*

Famous-Barr, as it became known, eventually grew to become the largest grossing single-location department store west of the Mississippi.)[95]

In 1896, May and the Shoenbergs turned their partnership into a corporation, the May Shoe & Clothing Company Inc., and continued expanding. In 1898, May landed contracts to provide the army with clothing for soldiers fighting in Cuba and the Philippines; a typical order included eighty thousand blue flannel shirts and twenty-five thousand pairs of blue pants. That same year, May Company added a third location after buying out Hall & Dutton in Cleveland (renaming it May Company). In 1899, May established a headquarters and buying office in New York, at 722 Broadway. The building, which still stands, was home to the May Company's buyers when they came to the city, as well as textile workers who manufactured goods for the stores. The proudly city-boosting *Denver Times* opined that this building in far-away New York City contributed "not a little to the fame of Denver." By growing his company so quickly, May become well known, so much so that President William McKinley offered him a post as U.S. consul in Frankfort-am-Main, Germany. The merchant gave his regrets—he was too busy building his empire.[96]

Despite traveling frequently, for a time May continued living in Denver. His family had first lived at 2546 Champa Street, but by the later 1890s, they called home a mansion at 2135 East Colfax Avenue; in 1900, May bought the Horace Bennett mansion at 1304 Logan Street. May was a towering figure in Denver's Jewish community and had good relations with Rabbi William S. Friedman of Temple Emanuel. One of the rabbi's great projects was establishing a hospital for sufferers of tuberculosis and other lung ailments. In 1901, May, along with fellow merchants Edward T. Monash of the Fair and Leopold S. Guldman of Golden Eagle, helped found the National Jewish Hospital for Consumptives at East Colfax Avenue and Colorado Boulevard, an institution that today is ranked as the leading lung research hospital in America. To the ends of their lives, May; his son, Morton; and nephew Alfred Triefus were closely associated with National Jewish, giving vast sums to fund the hospital's building programs.[97]

The new century brought yet more expansion. In 1901, the May Company purchased M. O'Neill of Akron, Ohio, and two years later, David May moved with his family to St. Louis, to be closer to his various Midwestern operations. It was a Missouri custom to call successful men "colonel," regardless of whether they had ever been in the military, so May became known as "Colonel May," at least in the St. Louis newspapers. Denver papers tended not to use this honorific, perhaps in deference to Major Daniels, who *had* served in the military.

THE CHAMPA STREET STORE

The big news for May in Denver after the turn of the century was a move uptown. The sprawling Larimer-Lawrence store had been cobbled together, and it was time to consolidate operations in one structure for maximum efficiency and sales. Not only that, but with Denver Dry Goods enjoying great success at Sixteenth and California Streets, May felt the energy shifting away from the old business streets of Larimer and Lawrence. Champa and Sixteenth was now prime, so in 1905, the company bought the northern corner of that intersection and built a grand new May Company, four stories plus basement. The new May would boast more than 90,000 square feet of space, with 125 feet of Sixteenth Street frontage and 150 feet along Champa.[98]

With a $500,000 budget, architect Edwin H. Moorman was charged with "devis[ing] a style that would be distinguished from any other building." He produced an exuberant Beaux Arts palace, with a white glazed terracotta façade and an entranceway lined in dark green marble. The building's brilliant whiteness easily made it the shiniest, cleanest-looking store on Sixteenth Street. Inside were numerous innovations never before seen in Denver, including "moving stairs" to carry people from the first to the second floor—the first escalator in Colorado and the only one west of Kansas City, according to May Company. From white marble fountains, parched shoppers could partake of "ice cold mineral water" drawn from the store's own artesian well. Highest quality furnishings and fittings included two art nouveau bronze "electroliers" illuminating the main stairway, sculpted by artist August Moreau. These may have been of French origin, but the store made a special point of letting the city know that the new retail palace had been "builded by Denver capital after ideas furnished by Denver brain and erected of Denver-made material." The early December opening, "in many ways…of vastly more importance than a mere affair of state" (gushed the *Denver Post*), attracted a crowd estimated at twenty thousand people, "a swaying mass of humanity" turning out to see the new May store.[99]

For the next eighteen years, the building served the store's needs, but the urge to grow was never far off, either locally or at the national level. May Department Stores Company incorporated in 1910, selling shares on the New York Stock Exchange. David May retired from active management in 1917, making way for son Morton J. May, who had begun his career in the original Larimer Street store. But David May never quit looking for opportunities, and in 1923, he made the biggest acquisition yet: A.

May Company's Champa Street store (1906–1958) in 1930. *Denver Public Library, Western History Collection.*

Hamburger & Sons of Los Angeles. Now May Company was a chain of five stores, with an annual business "in excess of $100,000,000" and more than fourteen thousand employees.[100]

By this time, May's nephew, Alfred E. Triefus, oversaw Denver operations. As a young man he, like his uncle, developed lung problems, and May encouraged him to come to Denver for the climate. He started clerking at the Lawrence Street store in 1905 and became general manager in 1922. Ambitious and observant like his uncle, he noticed great changes happening on Sixteenth Street. In 1924, Denver Dry Goods (no longer locally owned, having been sold to St. Louis–based Scruggs, Vandevoort & Barney the previous year) added floors and opened its vast Tea Room. It was also that year that Neusteter Company, largely catering to more affluent shoppers, expanded into a five-story women's clothing emporium at Sixteenth and Stout Streets. Triefus responded with a six-story addition along Champa Street, which opened in the fall of 1925. Costing $1 million, the wing by William A. and Arthur E. Fisher Architects (who had also designed the Neusteter building) gave May Company a 250-foot frontage along Champa, featuring a show window arcade with more than 10,000 square feet of plate glass the store christened "Fashion Lane." As before, May Company played up its Colorado roots, advertising that even though the St. Louis and Los Angeles operations were larger, the Denver store was still the "parent" of the others. Again, too, May Company played up the fact that the store was built with Colorado materials and labor.[101]

David May was unable to attend the expansion's grand opening. Aged but always working, he passed away in July 1927 at seventy-nine years. He had been at his summer home in Charlevoix, Michigan, when he developed pneumonia after a severe cold, and he was no longer the young man in Hartford City who could cure his ailments by moving to Colorado. He oversaw one last acquisition just before he died, in Baltimore (Bernheimer-Leader). After this purchase, Morton J. May and the board decided to hold off on any further mergers in order to consolidate their position. This prudence probably saved them during the Great Depression, when so many stores went into bankruptcy. May Company continued its practice of carrying a broad range and deep inventory and of quickly marking goods down when they weren't moving. By these methods, it not only survived the greatest economic downturn in American history, but it also actually thrived. May was one of the few large retailers to pay quarterly dividends to stockholders throughout the 1930s.[102]

By the end of that decade, Morton J. May and his board sensed they could start cautiously expanding again. Rather than buy, however, they would build: in 1939, the company opened its first suburban branch, on Wilshire Boulevard in Los Angeles. The following year, it announced plans to expand the Denver store again, building a seven-story annex on Curtis Street, across the alley from the 1925 addition. The new May Annex, designed by Fisher, Fisher & Hubbell, was connected to the 1925 store by a 75-foot-wide bridge on floors two through six. May Company no longer favoring ornate architecture, the new wing was designed in clean Art Moderne style, with limestone and glass brick. It was also fully air-conditioned, another first for a Denver store. As with the original 1906 building and 1925 addition, May called attention to the Colorado labor and materials that would be employed. The May Annex brought the total square footage up to 261,000, and the staff to nearly one thousand people. At the end of World War II, May Company saw another period of expansion coming as soon as wartime building material restrictions ended and issued new stock to raise $15 million. It announced plans "to spend 'considerable sums' in developing retail stores in suburban areas."[103]

STRIKE!

As thrilling as this expansion might have seemed to shareholders and uncritical journalists, the company would soon have to contend with prosaic reality: dissatisfied employees. Postwar inflation was taking a bite out of ordinary workers' paychecks, and Denver May personnel, who had voted in their first union representation in 1942, wanted decent wages and raises that would keep their standard of living from slipping backward. On August 20, 1946, the first-ever strike against a downtown Denver department store began, as Local 454 of the Retail Clerks Union of the American Federation of Labor called a walkout. The local's representatives were stalled in their negotiation for a $26 minimum weekly wage, a 25 percent raise for all store employees, freezing of sales quotas and, most importantly, a closed shop (wherein all non-management employees would be required to join the union). May Company had made a counteroffer but refused to sanction a closed shop.[104]

Pickets appeared, and the union soon claimed it was affecting business. May Company countered that traffic and revenue were at normal levels and that most employees had not gone on strike—but a mere glance at the help wanted sections of the newspapers would tell a different story. Among the speakers at a mass meeting organized by A.F. of L. representative Samuel Meyers at the Municipal Auditorium were Mayor Benjamin Stapleton (whose expressed sentiments were neutral but who showed up because May workers were, after all, voters) and author Mary Coyle Chase.

In the strike's early days, workers had the momentum, but it shifted as the strike dragged on. There were small incidences of violence, with newspapers reporting smashed windows and stink bombs detonated inside the store (the union denied it, and the store never brought charges against anyone). With the crucial holiday season approaching, in November, May Company asked the Colorado Industrial Commission to arbitrate. On December 11, it ruled that the local had "made an 'untenable' demand for a closed shop." Union representatives shot back that the commission, lacking formal jurisdiction, ought to remove itself, because May, as a national company engaging in interstate commerce, was subject instead to the National Labor Relations Board—Local 454's leaders knew they would probably get a better hearing if they went to the federal authority.

The next day, the A.F. of L. threatened a general strike of all twenty thousand of its Colorado members in various unions. They attacked May's hiring of strikebreakers, which the company had done "in an effort to break down the economic conditions necessary for human beings to exist under the present economic structure." The once-liberal *Rocky Mountain News* would have none of it. In an editorial headlined "A Threat to the Community," the paper called a general strike "both senseless and needless—an attempt to put a gun at the community's head." Both sides generated much heat but little light—the average Denverite probably did not feel cold metal on her temple but also did not want to cross a picket line.

The holidays came, the strike continued and the situation remained unchanged in January, when the strikers talked to Mayor Stapleton, whose excuse for not mediating to help resolve the dispute was "I don't know of anything that I could do." It was not until the end of March, thirty-two weeks after the strike had begun, that the two sides were finally in agreement. There would be no closed shop—May won that point. Pay rates would be higher than what the union had originally demanded, there would be double time for holidays and sales quotas would be abolished. Meyers opined that the striking workers should be regarded "not as conquerors or victors but as something much better, as the unconquered." The agreement came as a surprise to many, and Meyers held that "perhaps the long and bitter struggle might have been avoided if certain anti-labor forces in the background had stayed out of the early negotiations." He was referring to May's Denver attorney, who had been lead negotiator for most of the thirty-two weeks. Progress came about only after Alfred Triefus brought in the Cleveland store's manager to negotiate with workers.

A Chain Run by Buyers

With the strike out of the way, Denver's May Company looked ahead to a bright future. It was part of a rapidly growing chain, still headed by Morton J. May, that now had twelve downtown stores and twelve suburban branches, with 3.7 million square feet of retail space altogether. The chain, now with Pittsburgh's Kaufmann's in its portfolio, had sales of $358 million in 1947 and was looking to make more acquisitions.

Despite its size, however, May Company was unusual for being decentralized. There was no one at headquarters buying the same product for all stores—individual buyers at the store level made all of their own decisions, which allowed stores to cater to local tastes. "The store buyer has the last word, and no goods are ever planted in his department without his nod," a 1948 *Fortune* profile of May noted. Further, "May regards the independence of its stores and the autonomy of its store managements with almost savage fetishism." If the buyer bought something that didn't sell, he could mark it down for quick sale—even if the store took a loss—making room for new merchandise. Chain executive Samuel Rosenberg told the magazine, "We don't figure the merchandise. We finger it." In other words, accountants might run some chains, but merchants, who knew their stuff, ran May.

Different May Company units varied in clientele, with some catering to lower- and middle-income shoppers, while others aimed for an upper-middle class patronage, featuring higher-quality goods. Uniting all parts of May Company, however, was David May's original retail strategy of stocking as much product as a store would hold, with a wide assortment and deep inventory. Not for May were spacious aisles and open vistas—the company believed "calculated clutter" induced people to buy more than they would have done in a neater atmosphere.[105]

In 1949, Triefus announced plans to modernize the Sixteenth Street store by installing seven escalators to connect all floors. This was part of a general trend, as the old stores strived to out-do one another in modernizing their facilities (recall that Daniels and Fisher had announced a similar updating in 1947). Five years later, in a "major addition to the postwar 'new look'" on Sixteenth, May announced the original 1906 building's façade, deemed too fussy for the 1950s, would give way to light gray mosaic stone. The design, by Raymond Harry Ervin and Robert Berne, was stark: a mostly flat, uninterrupted expanse of masonry, with no windows, except for street level display. Block letters forming the word "MAY" featured prominently on the corner, more of an architectural element than signage. It was the age of the automobile, with simplicity and legibility favored: a person driving thirty miles per hour needed to spot the store quickly.[106]

The *Denver Post*, under the pro-business editorship of E. Palmer Hoyt, raved about the changes: "Beginning with the new J.C. Penney store at the east corner of 16th and California Sts., there will be a three-block stretch of gleaming new buildings to rival the shopping section of any other city. From the Penney store, the shopper will stroll northwest past Gano-Downs, Neusteter's, Walgreen's, Three Sisters, Lerner's, and the May Co., all modern in outside appearance." Such was the desperation of downtown merchants to compete with the coming wave of suburban branch stores.[107]

May Company, as mentioned, was a force behind that suburbanization. In 1954, it opened its first Denver-area branch at University Hills Shopping

May Company on Champa after its 1952 modernization. *Denver Public Library, Western History Collection.*

Center on South Colorado Boulevard and East Yale Avenue and, a year later, announced plans for a Lakewood store on West Colfax Avenue, in Westland, a center co-developed by May. The two-story University Hills store (later expanded to three, with basement) opened in September 1955, as the thirty-first store in the May chain. It featured a second-floor restaurant with a panoramic view of the Rocky Mountains, the "Leadville Room," named in honor of the town where David May had sold Levis and longies.[108]

Despite the new branches, the remodeled downtown store continued to be a busy place. A survey by *Cervi's Journal* found 2,140 customers entering May's main Sixteenth Street entrance on Friday, November 11, 1949, between 2:00 and 3:00 p.m., and this pattern continued undiminished through most of the following decade.[109] But it came to an end on July 31, 1958, thanks to a sea change in downtown Denver retailing engineered by William Zeckendorf.

Part III

SHOPPING WONDER OF THE WEST

Chapter 7
ZECK

Shaking this sleepy, self-satisfied town into reaching toward its potential as a city took many more years and many more millions than we first expected…I was blocked in all my moves…until I broke from the established pattern of play by taking a gamble that solved two problems and set Denver businessmen agog. I bought the Daniels and Fisher store.[110]

FROM PARK TO PARKING

The most colorful figure in Denver's mid-twentieth-century history was a New York developer who came to town in 1945 with the notion that Denver, a sleepy little burg little-changed for decades, needed shaking up and that there was no one better than himself to do the shaking. William Zeckendorf had big dreams and seemingly a big ability to accomplish anything. His Courthouse Square project (built where the county courthouse had once stood) would take nearly fifteen years to complete, and the publicity-loving Zeckendorf garnered much attention from local media during most of that time. Eugene Cervi (*Cervi's Journal*) nicknamed him "Zeck," undoubtedly because a four-letter word made for snappier headlines but also because, despite his obviously gigantic ego and tendency to condescend toward Denver's old guard, he managed to endear himself to other powerful locals who were grateful that he ignored that old guard and built modern new landmarks.

Zeckendorf controlled New York City–based real estate management company Webb & Knapp, Inc. Extraordinarily ambitious and a brilliant buyer and seller of commercial real estate, by the time he was in his thirties in the 1930s, he earned an annual income of $40,000, an extraordinary figure for the time. Inspired by the grandeur of New York's Rockefeller Center, he quietly began buying cheap land, mostly filled with slaughterhouses, along the East River in Manhattan, between Forty-second and Forty-seventh Streets. Once he'd assembled his land, he announced "X City," a grandiose project of residences, office space and an opera house. X City never got built, however, because about that time, the newly chartered United Nations was deciding where to make its permanent home. The U.N. was about to choose Philadelphia or San Francisco, after having been housed in (unsuitable) temporary quarters in the 1939–40 World's Fair grounds in Flushing Meadows, Queens. Powerful New York figure Robert Moses knew of Zeckendorf's X City assemblage and persuaded him to sell the site to John D. Rockefeller Jr., who then donated the land to the United Nations. Zeckendorf made a profit of $2 million on the deal and was fond of boasting later that he could have made $20 million, but he had wanted to keep the U.N. in New York.[111]

In May 1945, Zeckendorf received a visit from Denver realtor Burr Brett ("B.B.") Harding. As Zeckendorf later described him, Harding, "a wraith of a man in a wide-brimmed Western hat," whose gaunt face was "a sight to frighten children and unsteady men," was a rogue operator, someone who was never "in the fold of the local satraps and the lowerarchy [sic] of their dependents and hangers-on," but who nevertheless had access to Mayor Benjamin Stapleton. Harding presented him with great opportunity: a full block of land in downtown Denver, owned by the city, fronting the main shopping street, ripe for development. The city had wanted to dispose of the property ever since the City and County Building had opened nearby in 1932 but, during the Depression and subsequent war,

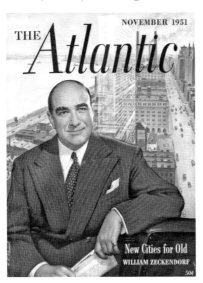

William Zeckendorf Jr., American master builder. © *The Atlantic (used by permission).*

Arapahoe (later Denver) County Courthouse (1883–1933), namesake of Courthouse Square. *Author's collection.*

was unable to sell it for anything like pre-Depression fair market value. In 1933, frugal Mayor George F. Begole wanted nothing less than $1.25 million for it, but there were no takers at anywhere near that amount. Hoping for better times ahead, the city demolished the old courthouse and maintained the block as a public park.[112]

Harding must have pressed the right button to pique Zeckendorf's interest, because word swiftly reached Denver that a big out-of-town developer wanted to buy the block and erect a modern ten-story structure that would feature a different store on each floor (such was the original plan). Interested in possibly developing the site themselves, local businessmen led by Lester Friedman (son-in-law to the late Leopold Guldman of Golden Eagle) formed a syndicate to buy the property, but once sealed bids from both parties were opened, Zeckendorf had won by a margin of $100,000. Although his $818,600 bid (up from an offer of $750,000 prior to Friedman's move) still did not match Begole's earlier estimation of the property's worth, Stapleton was happy with the deal.[113]

The citizens of Denver, who had not been consulted, were not. Despite the notion that had been floating around for decades (ever since Guldman had announced in 1912 his idea to buy the courthouse and build a department store) that the land could or should be profitably developed, Denverites liked having a park there. It had been public property ever since the county (Arapahoe, prior to the 1902 creation of the City and County of Denver) had purchased it in 1882 to build the courthouse. Its position on Sixteenth Street meant that it was well patronized by downtown workers and visitors, unlike the somewhat removed, more formal, Civic Center Park that fronted the City & County Building. There were no other places in downtown Denver where a person could escape the heat and noise, and the potential sale of the only green space in the entire downtown was proving unpopular.[114]

Citizens A.W. Hall, Mrs. E.K. Kalmbach and Mrs. Herbert H. Wooleson filed suit to stop the sale. This went ultimately to the Colorado Supreme Court, which initially ruled against Zeckendorf but later reversed itself. On the day following the reversal, December 28, 1946, the Denver Taxpayers Protective Association filed a five-thousand-signature petition with the court, asking that the block be preserved as a park, "for the benefit the public as a whole." Citizens Gordon Tamblyn, Lisbeth Fish and E.V. Graham then filed another suit on the grounds that the land value had risen to $2 million and should be rebid accordingly. But by mid-October 1948, all legal actions were put to rest when Judge Robert W. Steele ruled that the original sale price of $818,600 was indeed fair market value.[115]

In October 1949, a year after Steele's ruling, all legalities were resolved and Zeckendorf was given deed to property that had belonged to citizens for nearly seven decades. Two months later, he announced plans to turn the block into a revenue producer until he could start building. On January 8, 1950, a construction crew began removing forty-five seven-decade-old Chinese elms, thirty spruce and cedar trees, lawn and reflecting pool. They then poured a parking lot, downtown's largest by far, with a 364-car capacity. The city took Webb & Knapp's payment and put it into the Library Fund, for a new central library that Mayor J. Quigg Newton (who defeated Stapleton's 1947 reelection bid) was spearheading for the corner of Fourteenth Avenue and Broadway.[116]

A SECOND RADIO CITY

Zeckendorf did not park cars on the block for long and soon made his next announcement. He now planned a two-story "merchandising" building, on the Sixteenth Street half of the block, and facing Fifteenth would be an high-rise office building with a "transport terminal" at its base that would provide connections to air, rail and bus lines. Parking would be underground, and at the top of his skyscraper, Zeckendorf planned a suite of studios for radio and television broadcasting. It would be a "second Radio City," a western version of his beloved Rockefeller Center.[117]

Announcing plans with great fanfare was Zeckendorf's trademark. He called this the "optimistic announcement technique," presenting his plans to the public as a way of garnering support with the citizenry. He accompanied these events with architectural renderings and models of "towering buildings, moving sidewalks, [and] flower-planted and fountained malls." Faced with such a surfeit of fanciful imagery, the public could not help being bowled over by his vision.[118]

This plan came to nothing, however, and by 1952 Newton was "greatly disturbed" that the former city parkland, despite Webb & Knapp's announced intentions, was still an ugly parking lot. Zeckendorf blamed the Korean War, which had broken out in 1950, making both construction materials and financing for large projects hard to come by. In April 1953, he announced that construction would begin in 1954 on a Statler Hotel. A few months later, City Council threw a curveball by passing a new height limit on downtown buildings, meant to prevent airplanes from crashing into them. Zeckendorf's skyscraper, proposed at thirty stories, would be higher than the law allowed.[119]

Zeckendorf returned in January 1954 with a new plan for a shorter hotel that would not intrude into restricted airspace. More importantly, the project would now also include a new home for Daniels and Fisher, which he had recently purchased (as recounted in chapter 5; at the same time, he also purchased the Statler chain, to guarantee a hotel tenant). To realize this increased scope, Zeckendorf would expand the project across Court Place from the courthouse land to include most of the block between Court and Cleveland Places. Later that year, Daniels and Fisher signed a lease, and in November, voters approved an irrevocable lease to Webb & Knapp for the land underneath Court Place.[120]

Throughout, Zeckendorf faced naysayers. Gene Cervi, supporting him, opined in his newspaper that "deep-rooted in the tugging and

...napp, Inc., almost from the day it came
...e of the most important projects in the
...s, the faded dreams and aspirations and
...reof, that like hidden in the character of
...ot everyone shared Cervi's enthusiasm,
... old guard or his identification with
... because they'd visited other cities and
...d.[121]

Denver daily papers published breathless
bb & Knapp plan. Uncharacteristically,
 did not appear in person but sent his
:rom, to conduct the press conference.
$35 million to build, Rydstrom told the
ing facility, now a Hilton, would boast
ooms, instantly the city's largest hotel,
and would "somewhat resemble the slab-type architecture at the United
Nations Building in New York"—Zeckendorf never lost an opportunity
to highlight his connection to that project. Daniels and Fisher would
occupy 400,000 square feet on four aboveground floors plus a basement,
the "largest postwar department store west of Chicago." Webb &
Knapp knew building a store this large in a downtown area represented
a "complete reversal of the nationwide trend toward decentralization
of merchandising facilities" but believed that by building such a large
new facility, the store could anticipate a 300 percent increase in sales
compared to its original, now questionable, location. Most unusually,
the store would not front directly on Sixteenth Street. It would be set
back in order to make room for a sunken plaza with an ice skating
rink ("somewhat larger than that at Rockefeller Center in New York,"
Rydstrom promised, stretching the truth) that in summer would be
converted to an *al fresco* restaurant. Next to the plaza would be a third
building. Initially box-like, as his architect Ieoh Ming (I.M.) Pei worked
on it, this evolved into a hyperbolic paraboloid, a graceful, napkin-
shaped concrete structure with glass walls that instantly became a Denver
landmark upon completion.[122]

The buildings would be connected underground by a 1,500-car garage
("the largest privately-owned parking unit in the United States") and
above ground by a bridge. Construction commenced quickly thereafter.
Court Place was closed to traffic while the land underneath it was
excavated (the largest hole yet dug in Denver) and parking levels and

Zeckendorf's "second Radio City," complete with ice skating rink. *Bob Rhodes collection.*

under-street structure were completed. Blissfully unaware of what was going on behind the scenes, Denverites watched the project rise and imagined a future where they would park in the vast garage and ascend via elevators into a luxurious new Daniels and Fisher.

MERGER!

In August 1957, Zeckendorf's secret efforts to guarantee his project's success came to light. He had decided in 1956 that downtown Denver could no longer support three large, full-line department stores. It had the massive Denver Dry Goods, it had May Company and it would soon have an expanded and relocated Daniels and Fisher. He saw an opening in the cornfields of Iowa: Des Moines–based Younkers, which co-owned Daniels and Fisher, was feeling pressure from May Company, which had recently purchased an Iowa competitor. May, for its part, was concerned about what a relocated Daniels and Fisher ("a loaded gun pointed right at the heart of May," as Zeckendorf described it) would do to its Denver business. In a complex deal, Zeckendorf arranged for May to sell its Iowa operation to Younkers, so that Younkers could sell its Daniels and Fisher interest to May. At the same time, Zeckendorf and Younkers bought 9 percent of the shares in Denver Dry Goods parent Scruggs-Vandevoort-Barney and sold them to May as a deal sweetener.[123]

By now, Zeckendorf faced serious difficulties. He had to personally guarantee a payment to Bethlehem Steel for $700,000 so it would ship beams needed for the hotel. He had to appease a difficult new tenant, May, which was asking for substantial changes to the already under-construction department store—and May would not sign a lease or buy the Daniels and Fisher shares until its demands were met. He would also have to buy and later presumably sell the existing May Company and Daniels and Fisher buildings, and May stipulated that its former home could not be leased or sold to another department store (it did not demand the same for the Daniels and Fisher building, assuming no rival would want it due to its location). Cervi was concerned about Zeck's difficulties and editorialized, "Fading away in the harsh economic poker game are Denver's hopes for a smart, high fashion merchandising operation in the lavish setting of Courthouse Square. There is nothing in May Company history to indicate that it will operate the kind of really high class store that was envisioned when Denver voters generously gave Webb & Knapp an irrevocable permit to use the subsurface of Court Place."[124]

Zeckendorf managed to keep his poker game going. May ultimately bought Daniels and Fisher, creating May-D&F, and assumed the Courthouse Square lease. By July 1958, Denver shoppers were positively giddy about the store's impending completion. They had already enjoyed their first winter of ice-skating; the rink, christened Zeckendorf Plaza, had been dedicated

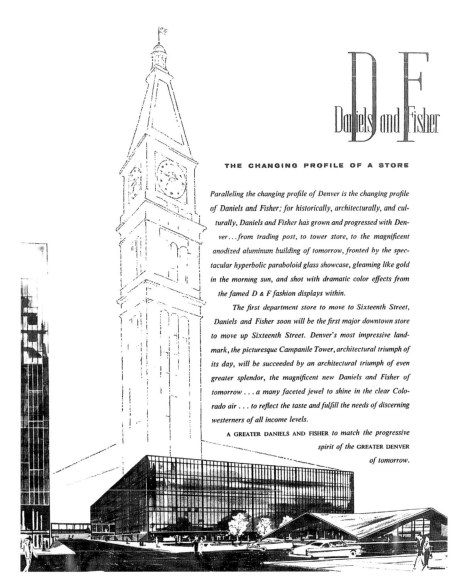

D F

Daniels and Fisher

THE CHANGING PROFILE OF A STORE

Paralleling the changing profile of Denver is the changing profile of Daniels and Fisher; for historically, architecturally, and culturally, Daniels and Fisher has grown and progressed with Denver...from trading post, to tower store, to the magnificent anodized aluminum building of tomorrow, fronted by the spectacular hyperbolic paraboloid glass showcase, gleaming like gold in the morning sun, and shot with dramatic color effects from the famed D & F fashion displays within.

The first department store to move to Sixteenth Street, Daniels and Fisher soon will be the first major downtown store to move up Sixteenth Street. Denver's most impressive landmark, the picturesque Campanile Tower, architectural triumph of its day, will be succeeded by an architectural triumph of even greater splendor, the magnificent new Daniels and Fisher of tomorrow . . . a many faceted jewel to shine in the clear Colorado air . . . to reflect the taste and fulfill the needs of discerning westerners of all income levels.

A GREATER DANIELS AND FISHER *to match the progressive spirit of the* GREATER DENVER *of tomorrow.*

Daniels and Fisher advertisement, July 1957, four weeks before the May Company merger announcement. *Denver Public Library, Western History Collection.*

the previous December with a big skating show by the children of Denver Country Club members.[125] A few days before the opening, the first May-D&F newspaper advertisement appeared, promising a "relaxed atmosphere" in purple prose:

Behold, your new MAY-D&F—Eighth Wonder of the World! It's a wistful wish come true…vast selection possible only downtown, *in a refreshing, leisurely atmosphere! You'll* feel *it as you stroll along tree-lined walks…pause at the skaters' rink. No need to hurry at MAY-D&F. It's all so big, so inviting, you'll naturally take time to* enjoy *shopping. Then, enter the Plaza Shop—most fabulous showcase on earth! Here is your dramatic* preview *of inside MAY-D&F. Moving on through the glamorous beauty of this* new kind *of store, you'll discover that shopping downtown is* fun. *Make a day of it…a shopping adventure in an exciting new world—your MAY-D&F. Driving? Our elevators meet you right under the store! Isn't it elegant?*[126]

Down Sixteenth Street, workers at Daniels and Fisher and May Company were preparing to say goodbye to their old homes and figuring out how they would harmonize with their former competitors once they were all working together. Joseph Ross had left in October 1957 after a fond farewell from Denver business and civic leaders to resume his Macy's career; sadly, he did not live long, his work habits getting the better of his heart. Mary Alice Fitzgerald would become assistant book buyer at May-D&F but would not stay long before beginning a second career at the Denver Public Library. From Daniels and Fisher came the odd announcement that cremains of William Bradley Daniels had been discovered in a fourth-floor vault and that they'd be moved to the new May-D&F. Shoppers jammed Daniels and Fisher during its final week, looking for deals and saying goodbye to the store that had loomed so large in their younger imaginations. May Company ran newspaper advertisements for bargains in the Champa Street store; the ads featured the old May Company logo at the top and the new May-D&F logo, with a drawing of the hyperbolic paraboloid forming the hyphen, at the bottom. In that first week of 1958, Denverites didn't worry much about the fate of either of the old "white elephant" store buildings, at least judging by newspaper accounts.[127]

The Shopping Wonder of the West Opens Its Doors

At noon on August 4, thousands watched as May Company chairman Morton J. May and his grandchildren (David May's great-grandchildren) cut the ribbon. Shoppers streamed through the futuristic glass-walled

Above: May-D&F utilized the hyperbolic paraboloid in advertising and packaging, such as this 1960s hatbox. *Robert and Kristen Autobee collection.*

Left: Early advertisements referred to May-D&F as "the shopping wonder of the west." *Author's collection.*

paraboloid to explore five floors of new wonders. May-D&F christened the paraboloid "Plaza Shop," stocking it with women's accessories. The main building's first floor contained a "block-long" (it wasn't quite) men's department, gifts, a Western shop, luggage, sporting goods, gourmet foods, a bakery and the clock and watch department. The second floor housed women's fashions, including furs and intimate apparel. On floor three, shoppers would find departments for boys and girls; teenage and infant apparel; the Fisher Shop for china, glass and silver; fabrics; and the Antoine Beauty Salon. The top floor featured furniture, lamps, radios, televisions, "high-fi" (record players) and major appliances. The basement was home to the Budget Store, "a complete department store in itself," along with a U.S. Post Office substation. As a sign of continuity with the traditions of the old stores, Carl Sandell, Daniels and Fisher doorman for forty-nine years and a Denver landmark himself, was there to open the paraboloid's heavy plate-glass doors for shoppers.[128]

What May-D&F did not have was any kind of foodservice—not a restaurant, nor a traditional department store tearoom, not even a snack bar—even though both Daniels and Fisher and May Company had boasted such amenities in their former homes. In negotiating its lease with Webb & Knapp, Hilton had managed to insert a clause forbidding such competition for its own restaurants.[129]

Cervi had earlier contended that May was unable to run a "high class" department store. While it is true that many of the decisions were made by

Left: Plaza Shop Christmas tree, decorated with hard candies. *Bob Rhodes collection.*

Below: Plaza Shop at night, viewed from Sixteenth Street, circa 1959. *Bob Rhodes collection.*

May people rather than Daniels and Fisher people, it was clear when May-D&F opened that it would be a cut above the May Company on Champa Street. David Saul Touff, who had overseen May's Colorado operations at the time of the merger and continued as May-D&F president after it, was charged with creating a special store, "the dominant store in the West," and his bosses in St. Louis gave him the budget and the people to help him accomplish that. They actively sought to dispel the image of May Company as a crowded, unlovely, bargain-seeker's paradise. While Denver Dry Goods and Daniels and Fisher had always outclassed the old May Company, with this new "shopping wonder," May-D&F stood a much better chance of dominating Colorado's department stores. May-D&F was tasteful and less crowded than the old May; its Fisher Shop for tabletop items and its Forecast Shops for "high-style" merchandise in various departments would have been out of place on Champa Street. Although some longtime Denverites never accepted that May-D&F had at least some "D&F" qualities to it, to less passionate observers, it was clear that May-D&F had succeeded in elevating itself above the old May Company, if not quite to the legendary Daniels and Fisher level.

The holiday theme in these early 1960s windows was "Candy Coated Christmas." *Bob Rhodes collection.*

Display director Bob Rhodes and staff artist Albert Gonzales often used the paraboloid's high ceiling to great advantage, as in this "Candy Coated Christmas" circus extravaganza. *Bob Rhodes collection.*

OLD DEVELOPERS NEVER DIE, THEY JUST FADE AWAY[130]

The openings of May-D&F in 1958 and the Denver Hilton in 1960 marked the end of Zeckendorf's efforts to provide provincial Denver with the trappings of a modern city, but his influence continued, as other developers recognized Denver's potential and began building downtown skyscrapers. In a speech at May-D&F's ribbon cutting, he gave what turned out to be prescient remarks about the potential for a pedestrian mall to transform downtown Denver (which came to pass in 1982, to a design by Pei Cobb Freed & Partners, the firm founded by his former in-house architect), but he also said that Denver was likely to be wedded to automobile transportation for the foreseeable future.

While he may have been a visionary, a successful businessman Zeckendorf ultimately was not. He had greatly overextended Webb & Knapp's resources in building Courthouse Square and simultaneous projects in other cities;

103

certainly his forced marriage of May Company with Daniels and Fisher was not part of his original plan. He was unable to obtain permanent financing due to his increasingly poor credit prospects. He tried to keep the plates spinning by taking on higher-interest loans but finally had to sell Courthouse Square to his creditor, Alleghany Corporation, to pay off the $20 million construction debt. He retained a master lease, requiring him to pay Alleghany an annual rent of $1 million, but by 1964, he had fallen behind on payments and lost his lease. In his autobiography, he blamed May Company for building suburban stores that diluted the positive impact of its new downtown showplace. His vast empire was crumbling, and he had taken out second, third, fourth and even fifth mortgages on some of his properties to keep cash flowing. He failed in the end, and creditors took over.[131]

In a 1966 interview, the newly bankrupt Zeckendorf was simultaneously proud and self-pitying. The interviewer noted that he still wore cufflinks created from gold found in the excavation for Courthouse Square. "I had some part in knocking the ball out of the infield for Denver," he boasted. "Sometimes only one or two buildings can change a city, and that happened in Denver. But Denver doesn't need me any longer."[132]

Zeckendorf gave a great gift to Denver in the form of Courthouse Square. Its construction inspired new hopes that Denver's downtown would not suffer the decline already apparent in many American cities. May-D&F greatly increased pedestrian traffic on upper Sixteenth Street, allowing retailers that lined it to thrive as shoppers made their way up from Denver Dry Goods and J.C. Penney. Capitalizing on proximity to May-D&F, Jack and Hannah Levy built built their four-story Fashion Bar flagship store diagonally across the street.

Zeckendorf did something else for Denver that boosted its status among large cities: he gave it first-class modern architecture. Whether it was innate good taste or just good for marketing, his hiring of I.M. Pei to design his Denver projects was brilliant. China-born Pei, a master of geometrical form, gave the project a level of design intelligence and classic elegance that became increasingly rare in subsequent downtown Denver developments. Despite Zeckendorf's massive ego, who could disagree with him, then or now, when he said at the Hilton's grand opening in 1960, "We leave you here in Denver a tremendous heritage"?[133]

Chapter 8

FASHION SHOWS AND FORTNIGHTS

This is a store keyed to the tempo of the Space Age, an architect's dream, a contemporary marvel…Denver is the heart of the West, a shining modern metropolis as inspiring as Paris, Rome or London. It is a city of culture, of symphony orchestras, museums, modern architecture, beautiful women and handsome men plus fine stores like May-D&F.[134]

THE NEW GIRL IN TOWN

In its new home at Courthouse Square, May-D&F was an immediate hit, and it thrived for many years. It certainly got off to a good start, with its ribbon cut by two great-grandchildren of David May, with Carl Sandell stationed at the Sixteenth Street entrance and with best wishes from everyone, even competitors. A Denver Dry Goods newspaper advertisement on May-D&F's opening day saluted "the new girl in town" in colorful phraseology (tinged with sexism, typical of the period):

> *We don't know how it is in other towns when a gorgeous new golden blonde (like You-Know-Who-Co.) bows onto the scene. Maybe in smaller towns, the reigning belles all fly into a tissy [sic]. Maybe in bigger towns, the gals get out their gold-plated claw sharpeners. But in Denver, it's different. There's always room for more pulchritude, we say. And we're dizzied and dazzled in admiration.* More power to you, May-D&F. *Anything that's good for*

Denver is good for us. Any friend of Denver is a friend of ours. We always say, if you're going to have a neighbor, she might as well be pretty. Hi, Beautiful![135]

As part of the previous year's complicated merger negotiations, May Company had agreed to buy 9 percent of the Denver Dry Goods' parent firm, so perhaps there was more to the advertisement than mere admiration. On the other hand, what was good for Sixteenth Street—a stunning new department store, complete with underground parking—*was* ultimately good for Denver Dry Goods.

The 400,000-sqare-foot May-D&F, with its paraboloid and ice-skating rink, became a tourist attraction, especially during the holidays. Not only was it the biggest store in Colorado, but it was also the first new downtown department store anywhere in America for several years, which made it comment-worthy. Unfortunately, it was also one of the last new department stores built in an American downtown. The trend toward suburban branches, which May itself had pioneered before the war in Los Angeles, continued unabated for several decades, and Denver, despite its wonderful new downtown flagship, was not exempt. In addition to University Hills and Westland, May-D&F opened stores in Bear Valley and North Valley in the 1960s, Southglenn and Aurora Mall in the 1970s, Southwest Plaza and Westminster Mall in the 1980s, Cherry Creek in 1990 and stores in other Colorado cities.

To compensate and to pull people downtown to shop, May-D&F promoted itself with gusto. In advertising, it highlighted the massive underground parking garage as evidence that shopping at the downtown store was just as easy as patronizing any suburban branch, and the downtown store, with its sheer size, could offer the shopper far more than any branch ever could. To build excitement and court the city's more affluent (and presumably more discerning) female shoppers, the store partnered several times with the Denver Hilton to present designer fashion shows in the hotel's ballroom.

Robert (Bob) Rhodes, a young man with department stores in his DNA, was responsible for staging these shows, along with many other aspects of May-D&F's visual personality. Growing up in Rome, Georgia (where his father co-owned a department store, Belk-Rhodes), he came west originally to work at an Estes Park, Colorado dude ranch but soon took a job as the "assistant display man" at the new May-D&F. Only twenty years old, he impressed management so much with his excellent window-trimming skills, honed at Belk-Rhodes, that when his boss Orville McCrea resigned, he became head of display (eventually he rose to vice-president of merchandising). His strong visual sense, especially the arresting theme and

May-D&F utilized the Denver Hilton's ballroom for fashion shows; in this Geoffrey Beene event, models appeared on different levels of the scaffold structure. *Bob Rhodes collection.*

holiday displays he designed for the Plaza Shop, attracted notice, and he became a well-known representative of May-D&F in local media. Assisting him was the talented Albert Gonzales, an artist who had spent his early years crafting stage sets and show cards for the vaudeville theaters that had once lined Curtis Street; according to Rhodes, Gonzales, working freehand, could craft and build anything Rhodes dreamed up.[136]

Two Grand Weeks

Like many department stores in that era, May-D&F also held special events, designed to not only promote products for sale but also imbue the store with a dose of culture—not highbrow, but more of a crowd-pleasing kind. Fashion shows were traditional for department stores—but two-week "fortnights" highlighting a particular country, usually in the fall (a traditionally slow period), were an innovation. In *Minding the Store*, his history of Neiman Marcus, Stanley Marcus describes how his store's 1957 French Fortnight, held in the downtown Dallas store, was inspired by a 1956 visit he had made to Nordiska, a Stockholm department store. The Swedish retailer had worked with the French government to produce a festival promoting French culture and products, and Marcus liked it so much that he decided to try the same thing, "an idea that has had a great effect on our business and on the many other retail enterprises that have copied us."[137]

Marcus gives the impression that Neiman Marcus brought to America the department store fortnight concept, which proved immensely popular in the 1950s through the 1970s, but he does not mention what his onetime protégé, Joseph Ross, did at Daniels and Fisher in 1955, a year before his Stockholm visit and two years before Neiman Marcus's first Dallas fortnight. When Dr. Guilio Bilancioni, the Italian vice-consul in Denver, proposed to Ross a celebration of all things Italian as a way of generating interest in his country, still suffering economically ten years after World War II, Ross immediately embraced the idea and created "The Festival of Italy in Denver." Held between September 18 and 26 (technically not a full fortnight), Daniels and Fisher partnered with Fox-Intermountain Theaters; the two for-profit entities conceived of the festival as a fundraiser for the nonprofit Denver Symphony Orchestra and Denver Film Society. Fox brought in actress Sophia Loren for an appearance at the store, and the retailer hosted a fashion show (exclusively Italian couture) at Belcaro, Lawrence C. Phipps's mansion in southeast Denver. Staged in Belcaro's indoor tennis court, models walked the runway as the symphony played. In addition to importing exclusive Italian merchandise, the store set up a replica of Rome's Fontana delle Tartarughe (Turtle Fountain) on the main floor and hosted an appearance by Clare Booth Luce, then United States ambassador to Italy.[138]

Building on what Daniels and Fisher had started, in 1960 May-D&F held its first fortnight, the Salute to American Creativity, celebrating American designers. It followed this up in 1962 with Salute Italia, like the 1955 event, another cooperative effort with the Italian government, but this time without Sophia Loren. The two-week festival of Italian merchandise and art included Italian sports cars displayed on Zeckendorf Plaza, strolling musicians, the well-known ceramicist Marcello Fantoni and a temporary espresso shop on the second-level bridge between May-D&F and the Denver Hilton (the hotel's lease clause forbidding May-D&F from operating permanent restaurants, as described in chapter 7, did not preclude temporary, event-based foodservice). Rhodes filled the store with Italian-themed decorations,

Right: Venetian gondolier in the Plaza Shop for Salute Italia. *Bob Rhodes collection.*

Below: Shoppers examine Fantoni ceramics during 1962's Salute Italia; note the large wall photo of the Campanile di San Marco, inspiration for the Daniels and Fisher Tower. *Bob Rhodes collection.*

including flags, banners and, in the Plaza Shop, an oversized Venetian gondola and gondolier, built in-house by Gonzales.[139]

The Wonderful World of Winter, arguably May-D&F's most elaborate fortnight, followed in 1964. This all-Colorado event was held in November, later in the fall than other fortnights, so that weather would be more winter-like (although it didn't turn out that way, with unseasonable temperatures in the seventies on some days). Colorado was then in the midst of the post–World War II skiing boom—the built-from-scratch resort town of Vail had opened two years earlier and would be followed over the next two decades by many more high-country resorts. Colorado Ski Country USA, a trade group, had organized in 1963. May-D&F had capitalized on the boom by

Above: A large crowd watches professional skiers emerge from the third floor and zoom down the ramp, during 1964's Wonderful World of Winter. *Bob Rhodes collection.*

Opposite, top: Publicity shot of Bob Rhodes (right) and an executive from W.O.O.D., Inc. in front of the Wonderful World of Winter's ski chalet. *Bob Rhodes collection.*

Opposite, bottom: Non-professional skiers could also enjoy the ski ramp; May-D&F president David Saul Touff holds the ribbon, and Colorado Ski Country USA president Steve Knowlton stands behind the girl. *Bob Rhodes collection.*

opening up ski departments in its stores, complete with skis, poles, bindings, boots and everything else required by downhill thrill-seekers.[140]

Partnering with Colorado Ski Country USA, May-D&F built a ramp from the store's third floor to the ice skating rink. The thirty-four-degree sloping ramp, twenty feet wide and eighty feet long, was covered with white nylon cut pile broadloom carpet, simulating snow. Professional skiers, employed by the resorts, made their way to the outside wall on the plaza side, where two of the aluminum panels had been removed to allow ramp access. With large crowds watching, they demonstrated downhill and rescue techniques. The ramp was designed so that the bottom could be folded back on itself to allow the rink to be given over to professional and Olympic skaters for shows. At other times, brave regular citizens were given the chance to try out the ramp.

May-D&F partnered with lumber trade association W.O.O.D., Inc., on a Swiss-themed mountain ski chalet. It was prefabricated, designed to be inexpensively replicated anywhere in the mountains, and May-D&F's interior design department decked it out as a fully furnished vacation home;

Extending sixty feet, the Wonderful World of Winter's Sixteenth Street windows included both animated human figures and mice. *Bob Rhodes collection.*

Sports Illustrated gave it nationwide publicity. After the Wonderful World of Winter was over, the building was repurposed as a home for Santa Claus.

Fashion was part of the fortnight, too, of course. The store hosted a fashion show in the Hilton's Grand Ballroom featuring designer Emilio Pucci's *après-ski* wear; proceeds went to the Denver Art Museum's acquisitions fund. Ski fashion for regular mortals was more the store's bread-and-butter, and one of its vendors, White Stag, was also a partner in the Wonderful World of Winter. Rhodes worked with the manufacturer to create miniature versions of its skiwear for the animated windows he designed for the Sixteenth Street side of the Plaza Shop (Look Skis, another vendor, created miniature skis).

Rhodes's windows received extensive press coverage. He designed them to reflect the Wonderful World of Winter theme and then be suitable for the subsequent Christmas season. He contracted with Silvestri Animated Display Creators of Chicago to build fifty-two miniature, moving figures, each approximately thirty inches tall, and his assistants created clothing for each. In the sixty-five-foot-long, six-scene "story," the first window on the left depicted vacationers arriving in Ski Country, with their car having

just overheated; the passengers moved on toward an A-frame ski cabin. The next section opened up the cabin's interior, with a family enjoying one another's company. The third vignette portrayed outdoor fun, with people skiing, sledding and skating. Moving past the front door, the right-hand side featured night scenes, beginning with couples on a hayride, indulging in romantic activities. The next window featured *après*-ski fun in the lodge, and the final vignette was a skating party. Throughout the windows, tiny mice, meant to entertain children brought downtown by their parents, reflected and commented on the human activities. Rhodes completed the effect with wooden trim for the paraboloid in an alpine edelweiss motif.

For the October-November 1966 fortnight, celebrating the cultures of three European countries, May-D&F came up with a portmanteau name: Festival FranSpaTugal, for France, Spain and Portugal. Like the 1962 Italian event, the store worked with the countries' governments to bring in artisans, designers and products. The previous spring, the buyers and Rhodes traveled to Europe, where they made contacts with artisans and small factories and took extensive notes and photographs so they could capture the countries'

Festival FranSpaTugal in 1966 celebrated France, Spain and Portugal. *Bob Rhodes collection.*

Festival FranSpaTugal's Plaza Bistro occupied a temporary building on the plaza. *Bob Rhodes collection.*

essences. Among the fortnight's featured elements were a thirteen-foot iron lamppost from Madrid, a collection of Picasso plates (retailing for $600), a Lisbon rug weaver and store windows featuring "character dolls," including a Portuguese fisherman, a Spanish matador and Napoleon Bonaparte. In the space between the paraboloid and the ice skating rink, the store built a temporary foodservice venue, Plaza Bistro, decorated by Rhodes with checkered, fringed tablecloths; copper kettles; French posters; and cobwebs, for an "old Europe" look. FranSpaTugal was not confined to the downtown store—the University Hills, Westland and Bear Valley branches also had themed displays and merchandise, and the French government worked with the Denver Art Museum on an exhibit, "The School of Paris," timed to coincide with FranSpaTugal.[141]

The Wonderful World of Scandinavia was May-D&F's way of inspiring Denverites to dream of better things in the troubled year of 1968. As before, the buyers and Rhodes visited the countries beforehand to capture the right feeling, and when the event opened to a loud burst by a five-hundred-year-

Above: Bjorn Wiinblad was one of many artists whose works could be purchased during the Scandinavian fortnight. *Bob Rhodes collection.*

Opposite, top: The 1968 fortnight celebrated Scandinavia. *Bob Rhodes collection.*

Opposite, bottom: Visitors to the 1968 fortnight dined at A Little Bit of Copenhagen. *Bob Rhodes collection.*

old Swedish cannon, followed by the Danish Radio Boys Choir, the city had two weeks to enjoy the cultures of Sweden, Denmark, Norway, Finland and Iceland—countries where color and good design were celebrated and were part of everyday life. The Hilton again provided the setting for the high society fundraiser, a *smörgåsbord* to benefit the Denver Zoological Gardens, with food by the executive chefs of Scandinavian Air Lines (a sponsor) and the New York Hilton. Shoppers could enjoy Danish cuisine at another May-D&F restaurant, "A Little Bit of Copenhagen," in a temporary structure facing the ice-skating rink, or they could take home Scandinavian food items from the store's gourmet department.[142]

With "Danish Modern" a popular 1960s home design trend, the store partnered with Scandinavian designers and manufacturers to feature the best elegant wooden furniture from the region. A Bjørn Wiinblad shop included

The toy department featured Lego during the Scandinavian fortnight. *Bob Rhodes collection.*

Scandinavian graphic designs decorated Men's Shoes in 1968. *Bob Rhodes collection.*

the whimsical artist's ceramics and posters, and another shop featured the sculptures and paintings of Bengt Carlin. For the kids, the toy department featured various Scandinavian dolls and a relatively new Danish toy, Lego (a then-Denver based company, Samsonite, had exclusive North American rights to the plastic building blocks between 1961 and 1972). In the plaza, car buffs admired Volvos on display.[143]

In 1970, May-D&F continued the fortnight program, returning to southern Europe with "Renaissance 2," combining those perennial favorites Italy, France, Spain and Portugal with a young country at the eastern end of the Mediterranean Sea, Israel. Once again, for two weeks that fall, the stores were filled with merchandise, arts, crafts, designers and demonstrations, with special emphasis on cutting-edge, contemporary designs.[144]

The last of the biennial fortnights came two years later in 1972, with Odyssey East, a celebration of all things Asian. India, Japan, Korea, Thailand, Taiwan, the then-British colony of Hong Kong and China were all highlighted (in February 1972, President Richard M. Nixon had visited China, so interest was high). The Plaza Shop featured a laughing, seven-foot-tall Hotei (god of fortune) from Taiwan and a Japanese garden and bonsai trees available for purchase. Inside the main building, Rhodes took a thirty-

Hotei, god of fortune, greeted visitors to 1972's Odyssey East fortnight. *Bob Rhodes collection.*

Odyssey East's fourth-floor Lantern Theater presented continuous entertainment. *Bob Rhodes collection.*

five-foot-long Chinese junk and converted it into a shop for newly available goods from the People's Republic of China. To board the escalator from the first to the second floor, shoppers passed through the mouth of a Chinese dragon. Artisans from Korea embroidered silk panels as customers watched, while in the children's shop, Japanese origami artists folded paper. The fourth floor featured the Lantern Theater, with daily performances by members of the National Ballet of Bangkok, Chinese folk dancers from Hong Kong's Miramar Hotel, Korean dancers and musicians (some designated "National Living Treasures" by the South Korean government) and demonstrators of traditional Japanese arts, including flower arrangement and kimono dressing. In addition to hosting about fifty visitors from foreign countries, the store also worked with members of Denver's Asian American communities to provide cultural demonstrations.[145]

May-D&F president David S. Touff resigned in 1969.[146] He had been the driving force behind fortnights, and after Odyssey East, they were discontinued. They were expensive to produce, so the payoff—increased store visits and higher sales—had to justify the cost. Luring the store's target customers (predominantly suburban middle- and upper-middle class women) downtown was becoming increasingly difficult, thanks to May-

D&F's growing fleet of branches, along with concerns about the urban environment, increasingly perceived, rightly or wrongly, as unsafe. This was not only May-D&F's problem, of course; other Denver retailers felt it too, as did downtown department stores in most U.S. cities. To new store leaders, the expensive fortnight extravaganzas were no longer considered effective drivers of store traffic—they generated interest but not enough to justify the expense.

May-D&F's themed fortnights, while part of a general department store trend, also reflected Americans' newly awakened interest in the wider world, as members of the generation that fought World War II were then at their peak of influence in American life, running government and leading private enterprise. Having experienced Europe and the cultures of the Pacific during and after the war, this was a less isolationist generation than its predecessors, and its interest in other parts of the world was genuine. Cultural historians could perhaps ascribe a patronizing aspect to these events, with affluent American consumers, in the tradition of world's fair visitors, sampling the exotic arts and cuisines of the foreign "other," without having to truly understand or acknowledge the hard realities of the cultures on display. However valid that argument might be in the context of world's fairs, it would be a stretch to apply it to May-D&F's fortnights. The retailers were having fun (and making money), but they were also fostering cosmopolitan awareness. People responded, genuinely curious and interested in what the store had on offer, culturally and otherwise. The whole community benefitted when May-D&F gave Denverites a reason to come downtown at a time when American downtowns were struggling.

American Spirit

The biennial fortnight concept may have ended after 1972, but there was one last hurrah in October 1981. The American Spirit fortnight harkened back to May-D&F's first 1960 Salute to American Creativity, but it may have also reminded those with very long memories of the intense patriotism of William Cooke Daniels, Charles MacAllister Willcox and David May. President Ronald W. Reagan occupied the White House, presiding over a generational and cultural shift. Instead of the spirit of worldly cosmopolitanism that had produced the first wave of fortnights, there was now, perhaps in reaction, stronger interest in American products and culture. The store's timing was perfect, and the event, celebrating the "pride, quality and vision that is uniquely American," was a hit.

The downtown store hosted 125 events over the course of sixteen days, and in some ways it was an even bigger festival than Wonderful World of Winter or Odyssey East. Four-fifths of the basement was given over to the event, along with about one-third of each of the upper floors. Among the highlights were a farmers' market; a personal appearance by chocolate chip cookie guru Famous Amos; Bob Speca, "the Domino Wizard," who spent most of the festival setting up 125,000 dominos that required forty minutes to topple; a Knott's Berry Farm shop; a flight simulator from Denver's United Airlines Flight Training Center, with the pre-9/11 public invited to try flying a commercial jet; a mechanical bull; the "world's largest sweater"; Bob Hope's gold tuxedo (and other items from the Paramount Pictures vault); displays from Colonial Williamsburg and Old Sturbridge Village; a professional Disney cartoon animator sketching characters for kids; a Smithsonian Institution gift shop; a scale model of the White House; miniature versions of First Ladies' inaugural gowns; Native American craft demonstrators; space gear from NASA; and, in a nod to the store's history, a replica of David May's original Leadville store, presented by Levi Strauss and Company. Instead of Odyssey East's fourth-floor Lantern Theater, there were spaces set aside for live musical performances on all five levels. Opened in time for American Spirit, the store introduced a new gourmet shop in the basement, featuring a wall of Jelly Belly jellybeans, reportedly President Reagan's favorite sweet.[147]

MARATHON

In addition to fashion shows and fortnights, the downtown May-D&F hosted other events from the 1960s through the 1980s. A series of smaller exhibitions highlighted non-European cultures, including shows of New Guinean, African and East Asian products in 1965–66. Also that year the store held a show and sale of ancient Greco-Roman artifacts, with prices ranging from $5 to $12,000. The Morton J. May Collection of New Mexican Santos was highlighted in 1968, and in 1972, the "Olive Branch Boutique" promoted Israeli pottery.[148]

Beginning in February 1974, May-D&F hosted an annual fundraiser for the Denver Symphony Orchestra (predecessor to the Colorado Symphony),

The outdoor Marathon Shop, in a custom tent designed to fit the paraboloid's roofline, sold items to support the Denver Symphony. *Suzanne Ryan collection.*

the Denver Symphony Orchestra/KVOD-FM/May-D&F Marathon. The idea to raise money this way came from KVOD radio's Marjorie Stuart and program director John Wolfe after hearing of similar events aired by classical music stations in Cleveland and Boston for those cities' orchestras. For the Denver fundraisers, which ran for sixty-six hours, the station brought its classical music library from its studios atop Ruby Hill to May-D&F and set up a broadcast booth in the Plaza Shop windows, facing Sixteenth Street (to the left of the main entrance). Marathons began at 6:00 a.m. on Friday mornings and continued until midnight the following Sundays. For a pledge, listeners could request any piece of music in the library to be played on the air. KVOD's on-air personalities, including station owner Gene Amole, broadcast during their regular times as passersby watched. Symphony musicians would join them for interviews and performances broadcast live from May-D&F.

May-D&F also provided a place where people could come to purchase Marathon posters (designed by Denver artists, including Vance Kirkland and Gene Hoffman), T-shirts and coffee mugs, along with various premiums donated by local merchants. These were sold in a Marathon Shop in the space between the paraboloid and the skating rink (where the fortnights' temporary restaurants had been built in earlier years) and rung up on the store's own cash registers, brought outside. The cold February weather was partly mitigated by a boldly colored, striped nylon tent, designed by Denver architect Peter Dominick Jr. to fit the paraboloid's roofline. Other non-merchandise premiums were available too, including a three-mile jog with Colorado governor Richard D. Lamm, followed by a meal at the Governor's Mansion with him and First Lady Dottie Lamm; dinner cooked by Denver's congressional representative, Patricia Schroeder; or a personal piano and violin recital by Maestro Brian Priestman and Concertmaster Jesse Ceci (for $2,500).

Marathons were true community events, run entirely by volunteers led (after the first year) by the energetic Suzanne Ryan, who coordinated over four hundred people during the weekends. Contributions came from ordinary listeners, many of whom had never once been to a Denver Symphony performance—many contributions were in the range of twenty to forty dollars. On a per capita basis, Marathons raised more money for Denver's orchestra than any other symphony marathon in the country, and each year the amounts raised grew significantly and always beat their desired goals; the event became the orchestra's largest single fundraiser. Conductor Preistman, in a *Denver Post* interview, said that people participated "for a zillion reasons, but mainly, perhaps, because it's become a symbol for a better life in Denver." [149]

The May-D&F setting was undoubtedly a major factor in the Marathons' success. Everyone knew the store and where to find it. A live radio broadcast in the store's windows added excitement and provided a sense of community. Classical music was not just for the upper crust, these events showed: it was for everyone. And they were also excellent examples of the kind of community support May-D&F brought to Denver in those years—not only the orchestra but also many other local arts institutions received financial consideration or donations in-kind from May-D&F. This would change.

Chapter 9

COUNTING BEANS

We're positive about Colorado's retail market—it's one of the strongest in the nation. It's just that the downtown store was losing $1 million a year and we have to run our business more efficiently.[150]

Too Much Space

The 1981 American Spirit fortnight proved popular, but crowds did not return after Bob Speca's dominoes were boxed up. Hilton's lease at Courthouse Square had ended, giving way to a new operator, Radisson Hotels, so May-D&F was finally allowed a permanent restaurant. Victorian-themed Denver Louie's opened on the fourth floor in 1977, with some of the aluminum exterior panels replaced with glass to give the facility (open for lunch Monday through Saturday) a view of the Rockies, similar to the vistas from suburban branch restaurants. Denver Louie's, seating two hundred, was named for Frenchman Louis Dupuy, who had operated the historic Hotel de Paris in Georgetown, Colorado. One of Denver Louie's signature items was a rich Monte Cristo sandwich.[151]

In 1982, May-D&F announced major remodeling plans as a "commitment to making downtown Denver a vital shopping environment." The Bargain Store would be downsized so the basement could be made over to resemble the popular "Cellar," developed at the San Francisco Union Square Macy's store. On the main floor, May-D&F reintroduced the Daniels and Fisher moniker for a "Brooks Brothers–style" men's suit department. Although this nicely saluted the store's history, the revamped department, emphasizing dressier, more expensive suits, reflected the clothing tastes of recently arrived residents rather than those of longtime Denverites and was not a great success. May-D&F chairman Larry C. Masters voiced what would turn out to be a vain hope when he told the local press that "if we don't modernize here, there will be no reason for people to shop here." He assumed a new, more contemporary look would bring back shoppers, but there were ever fewer reasons to patronize a 400,000-square-foot store when 125,000-square-foot suburban branches could satisfy most needs.[152]

In 1984, management accepted that gourmet jellybeans and oak parquet (installed over I.M. Pei's terrazzo) would not bring crowds back and decided the store could only be profitable as a smaller, suburban-scale operation. They contacted the Denver government to offer up to two full floors of leasable space—the city had more employees than ever and had run out of places to put them. *Rocky Mountain News* reporter Kevin Flynn reminded

Albert Gonzales recreated Theodor Geisel's "Cat in the Hat" artwork for a 1970s "Dr. Seuss, We Love Yeuss" promotion, shown here at the Southglenn branch. *Bob Rhodes collection.*

readers that were the city to take May's offer, "it would represent a return of government to the site" where the courthouse had stood. Downtown business interests were understandably alarmed by this potential downsizing, and while May-D&F president Joseph K. Davis told them the store "probably" would not close, he insisted it had 150,000 more square feet than it needed, and shrinking it was necessary. Eileen Byrne, retail project director at Denver Partnership (a downtown booster organization), clarified the rumors: "All that we had heard is that they would seriously consider phasing out the downtown store if development occurred in Cherry Creek." She was referring to proposed plans to redevelop the 1950s-era Cherry Creek Shopping Center four miles southeast of downtown into an enclosed mall, a project that would come to fruition in 1990.[153]

Another Merger

The city never leased floors from May-D&F, but by 1986, the downsizing threat was less important to downtown boosters than news that broke in June: May Department Stores Company was offering to acquire Associated Dry Goods, parent of Denver Dry Goods (by this time operating as simply "the Denver") and other chains, for $2.7 billion—the largest-ever American department store merger up to that time. The two companies had apparently been in "friendly and positive talks" since 1984, and with this merger, May stood to rival the country's largest chains. May was by far the more profitable of the two, with earnings of 4.6 percent of sales compared to Associated's 2.7 percent. In Colorado, the merger would knock Joslin's from the top spot—at the time, Joslin's annual sales were approximately $200 million, May-D&F's were $172 million and the Denver's $150 million. The merger briefly turned hostile when May's board grew impatient with Associated not immediately approving its first offer (May then lowered it), but by mid-July, it was settled as the two companies, with combined annual sales of $9.4 billion, reached final agreement. Over ninety-nine years, David May's little Leadville shop of 1877 had grown ("Watch Us Grow") into America's fourth-largest retailer, behind Sears, Kmart and J.C. Penney.[154]

Denverites wondered what would happen to the Denver, a beloved store with a rich history. Downtown Denver, Inc. president Richard C.D. Fleming said he doubted that either May-D&F or the Denver would close their downtown stores, despite all of the downsizing talk (the Denver had also proposed leasing out part of its space). May officials assured him and local politicians that there were no plans to do anything of the kind—May-D&F and the Denver would be run as separate divisions, even in competition with each other. They hinted the Denver might be repositioned more upscale, with May-D&F serving the broad middle. This fantasy lasted all of five months. In January 1987, May announced it would eliminate the Denver as a brand and either close stores or convert them to May-D&F, depending on location. This netted three new May-D&Fs, at Cinderella City, Northglenn Mall and Cherry Creek (which would relocate to the enclosed mall). It didn't need the Denver as an upscale operation—it was planning to bring Lord & Taylor (part of the Associated acquisition) to Cherry Creek.[155]

This didn't sit well with shoppers or politicians who represented them. Governor Roy Romer demanded to know why May refused to sell the Denver's locations to another chain, such as Dillard's (which had expressed interest in buying the division whole). Colorado attorney general Duane Woodard echoed Romer. "The bottom line is, is the May Company increasing its market share by nothing more than buying out its major competitor?" he asked and promised "closing stores and then arbitrarily refusing to allow any other competitors to enter the market through the purchases of those Denver retail outlets—that spells trouble." Mayor Federico Peña joined Woodard in a news conference, describing his feelings as "very disappointed." Soon, though, May sold the sites to J.C. Penney and Mervyn's—technically competitors but not as formidable as Dillard's would have been.[156]

Fooling the Customer

Perhaps May should have listened to the politicians. While the governor, attorney general and mayor had no power to affect May's plans to reduce competition in Colorado, they had other powers, and their dander was up. In November 1988, Woodard announced he was investigating misleading May-D&F advertising. He described newspaper advertisements claiming that certain items had been discounted "for a limited time," when in fact the "sale" prices had lasted much longer than a typical sale period, sometimes as long as two years running—the "limited time" wording misled the consumer into rushing in and buying a product before the price could go back to its fictional "regular price" (this practice is called "price anchoring"). Seven months later, in June 1989, the attorney general sued May-D&F for violating the Colorado Consumer Protection Act. He charged that May-D&F would establish "regular" prices by marking up the goods enormously for a brief period and then mark them down to levels typically charged by competitors. Further, in-store signage made it appear that deals were to be had, thereby discouraging shoppers from comparing prices at other stores.[157]

May responded predictably, pointing to its sales flyers and insisting that customers would typically visit other retailers to judge prices for themselves. In June 1990, a year after the suit was filed, it went to trial—billed as "the first of its kind" in the nation. May was found guilty of deceptive practices, but its fine was a slap on the wrist, a mere rounding error in an annual sales report: $8,000 in penalties, plus court costs, when May-D&F's Colorado sales were approximately $300 million. However, in making his ruling, Judge Larry Naves enjoined May-D&F from continuing to engage in deceptive practices; the store having already changed them prior to the suit's resolution may have been a factor in the low fine.[158]

THE END COMES

May was not finished disappointing the good citizens of Denver or its downtown boosters. Even though it had eliminated a rival when it bought and closed the Denver, reduced competition did not translate to increased business for the downtown flagship—without the sprawling, six-story Denver Dry Goods, there was one less reason to shop downtown. The company claimed the downtown May-D&F, the former "Shopping Wonder of the West," was losing $1 million per year. In early 1991, May-D&F announced that when its lease was up in 1994, it would not renew. Its Courthouse Square co-tenant, Radisson Hotel Denver, announced it would love to obtain May-D&F's space to expand the hotel, perhaps adding more floors.[159]

During the previous decade, downtown interests had hoped for a solution to the store's woes. In 1984, developer Oxford-Ansco (which was then erecting Republic Plaza, Denver's tallest building, across Sixteenth Street from May-D&F) proposed Centerstone, a two-block enclosed mall, running along Sixteenth Street between Tremont and Welton Streets; it would have been a simple matter to connect May-D&F as a mall anchor with a second-floor bridge across Tremont. Even with a city subsidy, however, Centerstone never got built—a new developer took over but lost interest, recession left other potential anchors uninterested and Cherry

Creek Shopping Center's owners announced plans for their enclosed mall (which garnered crucial political support). There would be no salvation for the downtown May-D&F.[160]

The end came sooner than expected. On January 28, 1993, May announced a cost-cutting reorganization that would combine operations of May-D&F with another division, Houston-based Foley's. Heedless of May's own history, this would erase the venerable names of May, Daniels and Fisher from the Denver landscape and replace them with a Texas transplant. Further, because there was no sense in re-branding the money-losing downtown store with expensive signage, the chain announced it would close a year early. About 500 office workers and another 250 from May-D&F's distribution center received pink slips. May president Thomas A. Hays tried to spin the news positively. "The May-D&F name that many people in Colorado have come to love and be comfortable with is gone," he said, "but we don't want people to think we're abandoning Colorado because we're changing our name and closing the downtown Denver store." "We still want your money" were five words he left unsaid.[161]

Main floor Christmas shopping in the 1960s, viewed from an escalator. *Denver Public Library, Western History Collection.*

Given May's recent history of negative news, politicians' reactions were predictably resigned. Mayor Wellington Webb said he was "very disappointed." Webb's aide David Gaon was more direct: "How they do business has got to leave a bad taste in people's mouths…they are not experts in building up good will." Retail analyst Linda Morris explained how May had evolved into the opposite of what it had been five decades earlier, when *Fortune* had profiled it: "May did not let the merchant side run the company. They let the business people run it." Local real estate broker Tom Mathews called May "one of the last absolutely dictatorially run companies"—clearly, no longer a "buyer-run company." Now, the merchandise was never "fingered," as it had been in the days of David and Morton J. May—it was only "figured."[162]

Liquidation began on April 13, and swiftly depleted of goods, the store closed its doors on April 27. In its last days, huge crowds came to visit one last time the vast retail emporium that had opened with such high hopes in 1958. The store's landlord, Gary-Williams, reopened the doors briefly, to allow three thousand young people, in Denver that summer for Pope John Paul II's World Youth Day, to sleep on the floor. Eventually the Radisson's notion of using the building for a hotel expansion became a reality under a new operator, Adam's Mark (this unfortunate tale is told in the epilogue).[163]

The May Company story continued for only eleven years after the Sixteenth Street store closed and the branches became Foley's. Through the 1990s and into the new millennium, May continued to expand through further acquisitions—notably Marshall Field's. Eventually, however, anything that grows too much can become too large. May had lost its way when accountants and lawyers made decisions that merchants formerly made. When the entire department store industry faced the existential threat posed by Walmart, Target and e-commerce, it was time to combine forces for survival. On February 28, 2005, May therefore allowed itself to be bought by Federated Department Stores, Inc., owner of Macy's, creating a massive company with over eight hundred stores (after the merger, Federated changed its corporate name to Macy's, Inc.). For consistency, former May units were re-branded as Macy's in 2006.[164]

Denver and Colorado are poorer for the loss of May-D&F (and the Denver and, for that matter, Joslin's, bought by Dillard's in 1998). William Bradley Daniels, William Garrett Fisher, William Cooke Daniels, Charles MacAllister Willcox and David May: these were Colorado merchants serving Colorado people. Will their like ever come again?

THE AFTERLIFE OF LANDMARKS

With imagination and a flexible interpretation of his program, he could have retained a world-class Denver icon, intact. He could have made a statement that he recognized Denver as a unique place with its own history, traditions, and architecture…he could have given new life to an internationally recognized symbol of Denver. [165]

The story of Daniels and Fisher and May-D&F would not be complete without recounting the fate of their landmark buildings.

May Company

The empty May Company buildings at Sixteenth and Champa Streets were not landmarks, and if there were people who were sorry to see them go, they haven't left a record. Perhaps, had May not marred the 1906 building's beauty with its harsh 1954 modernization, people might have mourned its passing. May, in its agreement with Courthouse Square developer Webb & Knapp, forbade its reuse as a department store, so options were limited. William Zeckendorf did not really want the property, an impediment to his already-strained cash flow, and when surveyors discovered a problem with the property line, he cancelled the transaction, keeping it in the hands of May Company. It remained empty for about two years after the store vacated—until 1960, when the Denver division of defense contractor Martin Company leased the 1940 annex for 1,500 engineering and office employees until permanent office space was made ready elsewhere.[166]

At the other (Seventeenth Street) end of the block from May's 1906 building stood Colorado National Bank. In the 1960s, the bank decided its immediate vicinity had deteriorated somewhat, and the block would make an ideal redevelopment opportunity. It began buying properties and demolished them all by 1965. After constructing its new headquarters tower at Seventeenth and Curtis, it had planned a second tower on the former May site, but nothing came of it. The May and other properties remained as surface parking for three decades, until a large parking garage, with retail space on the ground floor, replaced the lot in 1999.[167]

Daniels and Fisher

The fate of the Daniels and Fisher building and its landmark tower is one of the most drawn-out, convoluted tales of historic preservation in Colorado history, playing out over a quarter century. Comprising a full half-block, Daniels and Fisher was vast, 400,000 square feet on five floors of interconnected buildings deemed obsolete. It may have lacked such crucial twentieth-century innovations as air conditioning, but its façade was noble—as William Cooke Daniels had intended—and there was that iconic tower. Finding a new use for it after the store closed exhausted the energies of many men and women, and for some years, there was no real assurance that someone wouldn't tear it down. That we can still admire it today testifies to the labor of dedicated individuals, as well as to citizens' collective will to prevent the most important symbol of downtown Denver from going the way of so many lost buildings.

As with the May Company property, Webb & Knapp was charged with buying the complex from May, but here, Zeckendorf was unable to avoid doing so. Boulder financier Allen J. Lefferdink was the first to see the building's possibilities, and the last of Daniels and Fisher's merchandise had barely made it out the door when he announced his plans on August 1, 1958. He envisioned the property (renamed "Allen Tower Building," for himself) as a busy merchandise mart, where scores of wholesale firms could set up shop. His mart would offer space for seasonal trade shows, collective marketing and dining facilities. He claimed he already had commitments for 30 percent of the space and promised the mart would open by early 1959, planning to lease the building from Webb & Knapp until he could eventually purchase it.[168]

Lefferdink retained control of the building until October 1960. He issued stock and engaged contractors to install updated systems, build out tenants' spaces and give the building a good cleaning. To create the illusion of progress, he made Zeckdendorf-like dramatic announcements, including a projected 440-million candlepower beacon for the top of the tower. He made a down payment to Webb & Knapp, with an agreement to make quarterly installments until the mortgage was paid, but aside from one funds transfer, few of his contractors—or Webb & Knapp—got much money.[169]

Unraveling Lefferdink's dozens of overlapping and interconnected businesses—simultaneously with Allen Tower, he was building an amusement park near Golden, among other ventures—would have been a job worthy of Enron's post-meltdown auditors. It's beyond the scope of this story to delve deeply (a grand jury took on that task in 1961). His troubles stemmed from "check kiting," the practice of transferring funds from one entity to another to make it look like the business receiving the money was viable. But when one person controls all parties to transactions, eventually the scheme collapses. Lawsuits erupted, and funds were garnished. District Judge Saul Pinchick took control away from Lefferdink and placed the building in the hands of a receiver, Denver attorney Fred M. Winner.[170]

Winner couldn't win. Faced with negative publicity surrounding Lefferdink and grand plans left unfinished, the few tenants moved out. By early 1961, Winner asked the court's permission to borrow $100,000 to keep the doors open and attract new tenants. He was able to obtain funds and soldier on, but that was before the grand jury indicted Lefferdink and before the building went to auction in 1963. Rapidly crumbling Webb & Knapp had assigned its rights to Chemical Bank of New York, and Chemical was the only bidder at auction. By the end of September 1965, Winner declared the building closed, ordering the power and water turned off and the doors locked.[171]

Someone didn't want to leave. William S. Pierson had earlier moved his KBPI-FM radio station into the tower and possessed a signed lease he claimed was still valid, building shut down or not. He couldn't stand the thought that the clock, which he called "Denver's version of Big Ben," would stop, so every day he climbed 394 steps to keep it wound. With power and water back on, he was persistent as a tenant, continuing to utilize the tower as a signal transmitter until 1970 (when power was again disconnected), inspiring Denverites with his determination that the tower could still be integral to city life.[172]

With the tower officially closed, people came forward with ideas. The most fanciful emanated from Thomas Hornsby Ferril, poet and publisher of the *Rocky Mountain Herald*, a weekly paper filled with legal notices and interesting historical tidbits, who mused the tower would make a great "sky-scraping ruin companionable to owls and bats, with eerie vines creeping up the walls to entangle the hands of the great clock." He concluded that such a romantic notion could never come to fruition because "Denver has no imagination."[173]

Tangled knots of conflicting claims kept anything from happening. While Chemical owned the main building, different entities claimed other parts, including the heirs of John Alkire, who owned land underneath the tower. Chemical wanted to sell—they never really wanted it, buying it only to protect their claim to money due from Webb & Knapp—but couldn't, because there was no route to free and clear title. Neither the Alkires nor Chemical were opposed to converting the land to parking. Meanwhile, Webb & Knapp had subleased the building in 1963 to Younker Brothers, the Des Moines store that had been co-owned by Daniels and Fisher, but it wouldn't pay rent to the Alkire heirs because Lefferdink could still have a claim. The Alkires therefore sued Younkers. On top of everything, back taxes were owed to the city—no one was paying them. Pierson, meanwhile, wanted to pay rent to someone but couldn't determine to whom—he *had* to stay there, he said, because the Federal Communications Commission had licensed KBPI to broadcast from the corner of Sixteenth and Arapahoe Streets, and he didn't want to go through re-licensing to move the transmitter.[174]

Solving this puzzle became more urgent once Denver voters approved the Skyline Urban Renewal Plan in 1967. Skyline was the scheme of the Denver Urban Renewal Authority (DURA) for turning thirty-seven downtown blocks (later reduced to twenty-seven) into a modern, economically productive environment, ridding the city of its skid row. DURA planned to demolish more than 90 percent of the buildings in the plan area and re-sell the land to developers at low cost; Daniels and Fisher stood near its geographic center. In 1969, DURA gained control of the Daniels and Fisher properties after negotiating with each of the stakeholders separately. Shortly afterward, the Denver Landmarks Commission convinced city council to designate the tower an official historic landmark. This was followed by a second designation, a listing on the National Register of Historic Places.[175]

Empty Daniels and Fisher with KPBI transmitter, circa 1964. *Denver Public Library, Western History Collection.*

DURA had a massive renovation project on its hands, which did not fit with its usual way of doing business—assembling full-block parcels for developers was its forte. As events would show, the agency's learning curve would be high. To its credit, DURA proceeded with caution, making careful seismograph studies to determine the tower's stability once it stood alone. However, DURA never considered keeping the entire Daniels and Fisher complex intact. When the store was demolished over the winter of 1970–71, workers were careful to preserve ornate terra cotta and bricks from the Sixteenth Street façade so they could be used on the raw sides where the store had been ripped away (these were stacked next to the tower for several years but ultimately were not used). Once demolition was complete, DURA published a request for proposals and received nine responses. The agency assumed it could just choose one. It didn't reckon on having to through the process four more times.[176]

The first winning plan, in 1971 by Skyline National Bank (chartered to serve minorities), would have placed a banking lobby in the tower's basement and underneath adjacent land. The bank tried for two years to get the project going before merging with United Bank (previously known as United States National Bank), which preferred more conventional space. In 1973, DURA awarded Tower Square Associates (a partnership of Hensel-Phelps Construction and commercial realtor Van Schaack & Company) rights to the tower project, but this group walked away in late 1974.[177]

Denver's preservationist community was beginning to worry. Plywood coverings on the tower's sides were not holding up, and DURA was not keeping the building in good shape. Parts were going missing, including the elegant bronze entry doors. There were calls to tear it down, particularly by the *Denver Post*'s editorial page editor Robert Pattridge, as an un-economic, un-renovatable white elephant.[178]

The third plan, announced in January 1975 by a partnership called Luff-McOg, included a large exterior service core built on to the side of the tower up to the fourteenth floor, destroying the original Sterner and Williamson design. Geologist Kenneth Luff and the principals of McOg Architecture, who had been involved with the previous Tower Square proposal, planned to sell each floor as an office condominium. Stephen H. Hart, the state preservation officer and head of the Colorado Historical Society, filed suit to stop the ill-conceived plan, and it went through the courts. Luff-McOg lost the suit and appealed the decision but then decided to walk.[179]

In December 1977, DURA announced a fourth winning plan by Denver developer Louise Vigoda, who saw an unmet need for the sort of urban loft dwellings that were proving popular in other cities and planned to make each floor a residential condominium. Unfortunately for Vigoda, DURA awarded development rights for the remainder of the block to First Hawaiian Development Corporation, whose planned hotel would have blocked the

Daniels and Fisher Tower, centerpiece of the Skyline Urban Renewal Plan. *Denver Public Library, Western History Collection.*

tower's mountain views. Not wise to DURA's political side, Vigoda publicly criticized First Hawaiian and asked that it redesign its project. Less than a week later, DURA revoked her development rights, and she spent the next year and a half fighting DURA in the courts and in the media, to no avail.[180]

In the first months of 1979, DURA announced the fifth, finally successful plan to renovate the Daniels and Fisher Tower. Denver native David A. French said he was less interested in profit than in saving the tower for the city. A colorful figure who drove a 1933 fire engine in parades, French presented his proposal to DURA wearing a Santa Claus suit he wore for Denver's annual holiday Parade of Lights. He truly was Santa Claus to the

Daniels and Fisher Tower, appearing when it seemed DURA would never find someone who could successfully finance such an unusual project and please historic preservationists at the same time. Similar to Luff-McOg's program but without the external service core, French renovated the tower into office condominiums. His renovation architect, Gensler & Associates, designed new stairs, elevators and restrooms to meet modern codes. Work began in early 1980 and was completed about a year later.[181]

Since then, further work has been done, led by Richard Hentzell, a passionate history buff and head of the tower's condominium association and preservation foundation. Working with architects David Owen Tryba (whose firm occupied space in the tower before relocating to the William Garrett Fisher Mansion) and William M. Moon, Hentzell has spearheaded numerous improvements, including a new paint scheme, floodlights, dome re-gilding and flagpole restoration. The association contracted with historic painting specialist Grammar of Ornament to restore lobby ceiling frescoes, found antique bronze doors to replace the originals that had vanished under DURA's stewardship, replicated bronze light fixtures and curated a historical display in the lobby. The basement, extended northwestward past the tower's footprint to the property line, houses a nightclub, Lannie's Clocktower Cabaret, and the topmost floors are now Clocktower Events, a venue for weddings and other occasions. Since the mid-2000s, every April for the annual Doors Open Denver celebration, the public has been allowed entry, and curious multitudes have ascended to the upper floors, stepping out onto balconies to admire the views that William Cooke Daniels gave as a gift to the city more than a century ago.[182]

May-D&F

How different was the fate of the one-time "Shopping Wonder of the West." When in 1991 May-D&F first announced its intention to close in 1994, Courthouse Square's owner (since 1976) Gary-Williams Company worked with commercial real estate brokers to determine reuse possibilities. Gary-Williams announced in 1993 that the iconic hyperbolic paraboloid would have to come down because it could not be "functionally, aesthetically, or economically incorporated into a viable redevelopment program compatible with contemporary design standards." However, a year later, the same Gary-Williams announced it would spend $200,000 to repair the paraboloid's deteriorating roof and fix problems with its nine-thousand-square-foot interior space so it could be used for special events. It planned to divide the main department store building evenly between retail and office uses.[183]

Just a few months later, before any money had been spent, Gary-Williams sold the entire complex for $37 million to HBE Corporation of St. Louis, privately held by Fred Kummer, whose primary interest was operating and expanding his Adam's Mark hotel chain. Kummer asked the city to close Court Place between the original hotel and the vacant May-D&F so he could build a lobby to connect both buildings. He planned to add more floors on to the store building, creating a 1,100-room convention headquarters hotel, something Denver's business and civic leaders had been urgently wanting. The new Colorado Convention Center had opened in 1990, but booking large conventions was proving difficult. The city believed more hotel rooms would help, particularly in a facility with a four-digit room count. The hyperbolic paraboloid, Kummer announced, would host a nightclub for "well-dressed" younger people. If the city refused to close Court Place, Kummer threatened, he'd still buy and renovate the existing hotel but wouldn't expand it into the May-D&F building, leaving it vacant and deteriorating. Kummer asked DURA for a $30 million subsidy to help finance his plan.[184]

A few weeks later, Mayor Wellington Webb announced the city would not consider closing Court Place. HBE then announced it would buy the full two-block property anyway, but the paraboloid would be demolished to make room for the hotel's coffee shop, fine dining restaurant and sports bar. Webb said he was not concerned about saving the paraboloid but was instead focused solely on making the convention center work economically: "I feel very pleased. We have a developer who wants to build a 1,000-room hotel that will help us get many more conventions." Downtown Denver, Inc. decided it would back Kummer and publicly opposed the Denver Landmarks Commission, which favored declaring Zeckendorf Plaza (the skating rink) and hyperbolic paraboloid as landmarks. Bill Mosher, president of the downtown booster group, said his organization would prefer to see the paraboloid stay, but "it is more of an urban design issue and not a historic preservation issue." Kummer's Denver law firm argued that the Courthouse Square project (the paraboloid in particular) wasn't really the work of I.M. Pei anyway, as he was not listed as the project's principal architect—Harry Cobb, his longtime partner, was. The implied reasoning was that if it were truly

Pei's design, it was somehow more deserving of preservation than Cobb's work (Cobb has many accolades of his own—he's just not as well known by the general public as Pei).[185]

Michael Paglia, art and architecture critic for alternative newsweekly *Westword*, and Mary Voelz Chandler, who filled the same role at the *Rocky Mountain News*, were passionate fans of Pei's Courthouse Square design, and both attacked the argument in several columns. Paglia described a Denver Landmarks Commission hearing held on April 18, 1995, with members of Denver's historic preservation community and Kummer's lawyers. Testifying was Denver architect Alan Golin Gass, who had worked for the Pei firm during Courthouse Square's construction. Preparing for the hearing, Gass discussed the controversy with Cobb (Pei had retired), who corroborated Gass's memory that Pei had indeed been principal architect. While Cobb served as primary architect for the May-D&F portion and the firm's Araldo Cossutta for the hotel, Pei had led the team (which also included Eason Leonard, Leonard Jacobsen and Denver architect Charles Sink). Pei hadn't designed every piece, but the overall assemblage was his, and he had signed off on every element; he had particularly focused on the skating rink, a feature of which he was quite proud, as the only portion of the site that retained its openness to the sky and nature. Cobb told Gass, "The design team agonized over every element of the composition of Court House Square. The proportions of the store to the hotel, to the open space of the skating rink, to the paraboloid were a combination of careful measurement and intuitive thought. We arrived at nothing lightly. Further, there are no examples of a thin shell concrete paraboloid form as eloquent as this one, which makes architecture of structure."[186]

The need for a 1,000-room hotel was apparently so great that Denver's business and governmental powers circled the wagons, seeking creative ways to get what they wanted. The building sat empty as politicians and Kummer went back and forth. By the spring of 1995, pro-hotel boosters portrayed the Denver Landmarks Commission as acting against downtown's economic future. Webb, running for reelection, promised to work on saving the paraboloid. Kummer hired local architect George Hoover to determine if the paraboloid could be worked into the hotel's functional program. Hoover concluded it would be impossible, but it could be replaced by another significant building, an "elegant box" of some sort.

On Monday, June 19, 1995, eight city council members voted against landmark designation, with only two, Mary DeGroot and Bill Scheitler, voting for it. In *Westword*, Paglia was scathing: "To put a sophisticated work of art such as Zeckendorf Plaza before the Webb administration or the city council for their aesthetic evaluation is not unlike the legendary casting of pearls before swine." Historic Denver, Inc., led by Kathleen Brooker, urged the paraboloid's preservation, as did many others in Denver and elsewhere, including Pei's biographer Carter Wiseman, prominent architect Robert A.M. Stern and Denver's Modern Architecture Preservation League.[187]

In a later lecture, Gass articulated what many felt:

> *The stalemate over the redevelopment of Court House Square revolved around the reluctance of the developer of the Adams Mark Hotel to recognize that, with imagination and a flexible interpretation of his program, he could have retained a world-class Denver icon, intact. He could have made a statement that he recognized Denver as a unique place with its own history, traditions, and architecture. Such an attitude, I still believe, would have been a "win-win" situation for the developer and the City of Denver. He could have restored the lost activity and economic vitality to upper downtown Denver, and, at the same time, he could have given new life to an internationally recognized symbol of Denver.*[188]

In October, DURA announced it would sell $25 million in bonds to subsidize Kummer's project. The agency had been withholding funds until HBE's in-house architects could produce an acceptable design. Damning the result with faint praise, DURA executive director Susan Powers said, "We feel we've gotten to the point where the design is dramatically improved over where it was when it was submitted, and we're ready to move forward...this may not be the best design, but it's important to recognize that the process resulted in a better design." Curiously, although it never became a political issue, after getting DURA to agree sell bonds, Kummer bought some of them himself—he was in the peculiar position of collecting interest on money loaned to his own company, as Paglia revealed.[189]

Demolition of I.M. Pei's plaza/skating rink and hyperbolic paraboloid began in 1996, a months-long process that broke many hearts—Paglia compared it to water torture. In 1997, the "elegant box" was completed, along with additional floors, clad in bronze-tinted reflective glass. Many thoughtful observers panned Kummer's taste in (or complete ignorance of) architecture and design. A taxi drop-off took the place of Zeckendorf Plaza. The banal "elegant box," although expensively covered in high-grade brown granite, would have looked at home at any suburban shopping mall. In the center of the taxi turnaround, where living ice skaters once glided,

May-D&F's hyperbolic paraboloid, shorn of glass, during demolition. *Photo by Alan Golin Gass, FAIA.*

was Kummer's gift to the city (actually a required public art component), a grouping of elongated bronze ballerina dancers by a St. Louis artist, panned by Chandler as "Giacometti meets Pippi Longstocking." In contrast to May-D&F's grand opening in 1958 and the Hilton's in 1960, the 1997 Adam's Mark opening was not a source for civic pride, and most of the public barely noticed.[190]

The Adam's Mark, whose creation entailed the demolition of such a significant piece of Denver's mid-century past, did not last. By 2008, the chain had gradually shrunk to just four scattered hotels, and it dissolved. New owners reflagged the Denver hotel as a Sheraton and spent millions renovating guestrooms and interior spaces. There was nothing they could do about restoring the destroyed landmark—the damage had been done.

NOTES

Introduction

1. *Denver Post,* January 23, 1955.
2. *Post,* November 11, 1955, "Empire" magazine.

Chapter 1

3. Anonymous, *From Prairie Days to 1907: Being a History of the Daniels and Fisher Stores Company* (Denver, CO: Press of the Smith-Brooks Company, 1907), 1.
4. Parkhill, *Donna,* 20; *Denver Republican,* December 25, 1890; *Post,* October 6, 1907; www.genealogycenter.info/pdf/kansasmillington/ KansasMillington2Text.pdf, accessed February 1, 2015; *Denver Times,* January 5, 1891.
5. Leonard and Noel, *Denver,* 6–8, 24.
6. Ibid., 9, 11, 24.
7. Riordan, Marguerite, Papers, Denver Public Library Western History Collection, WH1094, Box 6, FF19, "Daniels and Fishers [*sic*]," unpublished manuscript, 9–10.
8. Ibid., 11, 14; *Post,* October 6, 1907.
9. Riordan, "Daniels," 17; Riordan Papers, "Material furnished by Mrs. Pierpont Fuller, Letters of Wm. G. Fisher to His Mother."
10. Riordan, "Daniels," 17.
11. Ibid., 19.
12. Anonymous, *From Prairie Days,* 6.
13. Parkhill, *Donna,* 21.

14. Riordan, "Daniels," 23.
15. Riordan Papers, "Letters of Wm. G. Fisher."
16. *Post*, October 6, 1907; Riordan Papers, "Letters of Wm. G. Fisher."
17. *Rocky Mountain News*, January 20, 1875; *Republican*, October 6, 1907; Anonymous, *From Prairie Days*, 7.

Chapter 2

18. *Rocky Mountain Herald*, November 7, 1896.
19. Anonymous, *From Prairie Days*, 10.
20. Ibid; *News*, January 1, 1878; www.davemanuel.com/inflation-calculator. php, accessed on February 8, 2014.
21. Some accounts of the change from two to four floors say the original foundations would not support additional floors and the building was demolished and rebuilt. This seems unlikely, as contemporaneous newspaper accounts do not mention it—only later accounts, written in the 1890s and early 1900s, do.
22. *News*, December 31, 1879.
23. *Republican*, October 6, 1907.
24. Anonymous, *From Prairie Days*, 14; Riordan, "Daniels," 46–47.
25. *Times*, December 31, 1897; *Post*, April 28, 1901.
26. The Panic was the result of a number of seemingly unrelated events, including the failure of the Argentinian wheat crop and railroad over-building, resulting in numerous bankruptcies not only of railroads but also other kinds of businesses.
27. Leonard and Noel, *Denver*, 103.
28. *Herald*, November 7, 1896.
29. Riordan, "Daniels," 39–40.
30. Ibid., 56, 59.
31. Ibid., 65. Given Riordan's propensity for colorful writing, this story could be apocryphal. However, in Frances Trott Robinson (Papers, History Colorado, MSS 529), her daughter Katherine Robinson Wilson in an unpublished typescript, "Eighty-Three Years Growing Up with Denver," mentions interviewing Charles Taylor, a retired buyer, who remembers "how Baby Doe enjoyed 'curb service' whenever she went shopping, as did many of the 'soiled doves' of Larimer Street. She would drive up in her coach to the carriage entrance and send her coachman to summon a clerk. Usually two clerks went out, their arms loaded with great bolts of brocades, satins, Henrietta cloth and British tweed. From these the beautiful bride of Tabor would choose the wardrobe that was to startle the town-folk whenever she sallied forth." Wilson was the granddaughter of A.B. Trott, a later co-owner of the store.

Chapter 3

32. Parkhill, *Donna*, 57. Unless otherwise cited, this chapter derives from that source; from *Times*, January 5, 1891, and December 2, 1893; and from *Colorado Sun*, July 3, 1892.
33. Prosecuting attorney John F. Shafroth, a future Colorado governor, recited this bit of poetry at Donna Madixxa's criminal trial.
34. Complicating the picture, some years later, Henry Mitchell sued Daniels, asserting that Daniels had "alienated the affections" of Annie.
35. www.davemanuel.com/inflation-calculator.php, accessed on February 16, 2014.
36. Ed Duncan, "A Denver Love Story...or a May-December Marriage," *City Edition*, December 14, 1983.
37. *Times*, January 5, 1891. The *Times* article does not mention which of its competitors was to publish the piece.

Chapter 4

38. Anonymous, *From Prairie Days*, 28.
39. *Post*, January 14, 1907; *Republican*, December 25, 1890; *Times*, January 5, 1891; June 24, 1900.
40. *Post*, January 14, 1907.
41. *Republican*, September 29, 1892; *Herald*, November 7, 1896.
42. *News*, April 25, 1897.
43. *Post*, April 28, 1901; *Republican*, September 24, 1901; *Times*, December 31, 1897.
44. Riordan, "Daniels," 95; *Times*, May 26, 1901.
45. *Colorado Statesman*, December 17, 1910.
46. *Post*, October 6, 1907; *Times*, April 16, 1899.
47. *Times*, October 11, 1899; August 3, 1900; August 9, 1900.
48. Ibid., February 3, 1899; April 24, 1899.
49. *Post*, March 29, 1908; *Republican*, July 2, 1905; *Times*, July 1, 1902; June 27, 1908.
50. *Post*, April 28, 1901; *Times*, April 28, 1901.
51. Riordan, "Daniels," 73–74; *Times*, June 22, 1901; July 29, 1902.
52. Papers, Charles MacAllister Willcox and the Willcox Family, History Colorado, MSS #1606.
53. *Post*, January 14, 1907.
54. *News*, January 14, 1907; *Post*, January 14, 1907.
55. *Post*, January 20, 1907; April 3, 1907; *Times*, April 3, 1907.
56. *News*, February 28, 1909; *Post*, February 1, 1909; *Times*, April 3, 1907.

57. *Post*, February 16, 1910; *Republican*, February 13, 1910; *Times*, December 11, 1900.

58. *The Hitchhiker's Guide to the Galaxy: Earth Edition*, "World's Tallest Buildings—A Timeline for the 20th Century," http://h2g2.com/edited_entry/A32873871, accessed May 15, 2015; *Times*, November 13, 1910, 3.

59. *Times*, November 6, 1911.

60. *Post*, July 13, 1910.

61. Willcox Papers, FF53, "Alan Fisher Short Story," sent by Alan Fisher to Elaine Willcox Odeschalchi in 1965.

62. Riordan, "Daniels," 78. Frances Trott Robinson told Marguerite Riordan that it was A.B. Trott who had suggested St. Mark's and that Daniels presented him with an automobile as a thank-you gift.

63. http://en.wikipedia.org/wiki/St_Mark%27s_Campanile, accessed March 15, 2015; *Post*, March 5, 1911, "Magazine Section"; *Times*, December 25, 1910.

64. *Post*, August 24, 1910; *Republican*, November 22, 1910; *Times*, June 15, 1910.

65. *Post*, January 1, 1911.

66. *News*, July 29, 1911; July 30, 1911; August 22, 1950; *Post*, March 29, 1911; July 30, 1911; June 10, 1954.

67. Daniels and Fisher advertisement, *Republican*, November 5, 1911; *Post*, November 7, 1911; *Times*, November 6, 1911.

68. Riordan, "Daniels," 99–101.

69. *Post*, January 22, 1918; *Republican*, May 22, 1912.

70. *News*, March 19, 1918; *Post*, March 1918; April 1, 1918.

71. *News*, October 27, 1918, 5; *Post*, October 27, 1918; September 26, 1955, 35C.

72. *Post*, April 1, 1918; December 31, 1918.

73. Ibid., September 26, 1955.

Chapter 5

74. Francis Wayne, "Daniels & Fisher Stores to Celebrate 65 Years of Service," *Post*, November 3, 1929.

75. *News*, May 21, 1922.

76. Fitzgerald, Mary Alice. Papers, 1948–1958, 1997–2002 (MS), Denver Public Library, Western History and Genealogy Collection, MSS WH1800. Oral history recorded January 1997, transcript dated December 10, 1997, interviewed by Jodi Blakeley and Maggie Postlethwaite. Among Willcox's collection were first editions of Pepys's *Diary*, Goethe's *Faust*, Dryden's *Troilus and Cressida* and Cervantes's *Don Quixote*; Riordan, "Daniels," 84.

77. *News*, March 3, 1929; *Post*, March 3, 1929.

78. Allied Stores Corporation, after being acquired by Campeau Corporation in 1986, merged with Federated Department Stores in 1988. Federated changed its name to Macy's Inc. in 2006.

79. Willcox papers: letters from Orlando B. Willcox to Charles MacAllister Willcox, August 7, 1928, January 22, 1929, February 13, 1929, and March 9, 1929; telegram from Eugene Greenut to Charles MacAllister Willcox, February 25, 1929; *News*, October 20, 1932; Michael Lisicky, *Shop Pomeroy's First* (Charleston, SC: The History Press, 2014), 45; http://www.library.hbs.edu/hc/lehman/company.html?company=hahn_department_stores_inc, accessed April 11, 2015.

80. *News*, August 24, 1930.

81. Ibid., January 27, 1939; January 30, 1940; January 30, 1945; *Post*, December 23, 1944; February 13, 1946; October 18, 1946.

82. *Post*, March 13, 1948; May 10, 1948; May 19, 1948; February 2, 1949.

83. Sandra Barnhouse, e-mail to author, January 13, 2015.

84. *Post*, August 1, 1950.

85. William Zeckendorf, with Edward McCreary, *The Autobiography of William Zeckendorf* (New York: Holt, Rinehart and Winston, 1970), 122.

86. *News*, May 23, 1954; *Post*, May 23, 1954.

87. *News*, November 16, 1954; *Post*, March 10, 1954; May 30, 1954; September 28, 1954; November 15, 1954; January 16, 1955.

88. Fitzgerald, Papers; *Cervi's Rocky Mountain Journal*, May 26, 1955, 1; *Post*, January 5, 1955; May 25, 1955.

89. Fitzgerald, Papers; *Post*, January 16, 1955.

90. *News*, March 15, 1956.

Chapter 6

91. Examples of early May advertisement headlines, quoted in *Post*, September 26, 1952.

92. Biographical details derive from *Fortune*, December 1948, 109; *The Mayfare* (employee newsletter), special edition, "The May Co. Celebrates Seventy-Five Years of Progress, 1877–1952"; *News*, September 13, 1925; July 23, 1927; April 23, 1939; *Post*, July 23, 1927; Forbes Parkhill, "The May Story," appearing in six installments in the *Post*, September 23–28, 1952.

93. May's meeting Field on this trip may be apocryphal, but it was mentioned in more than one account of May's life; *News*, April 23, 1939; *Post*, July 23, 1927.

94. *Mayfare*, 8.

95. Gravenhorst, *Famous-Barr*, 32.

96. *Times*, July 28, 1898; June 21, 1899.

97. Ibid., November 17, 1901.

98. *Republican*, January 7, 1906.

99. *Post*, December 2, 1906; December 4, 1906.

100. *Fortune*, 152.

101. *News*, October 9, 1924; September 13, 1925.

102. *Fortune*, 153.

103. *News*, November 19, 1940; March 5, 1945; July 23, 1946; *Post*, November 18, 1940.

104. The strike received extensive coverage: *News*, August 21, 1946; November 22, 1946; November 27, 1946; December 13, 1946; December 15, 1946; March 31, 1947; April 2, 1947; *Post*, August 30, 1946; September 6, 1946; September 26, 1946; November 21, 1946; November 22, 1946; December 11, 1946; December 12, 1946; December 12, 1946; January 7, 1947; March 31, 1947; April 2, 1947.

105. *Fortune*, 109–12.

106. *News*, April 3, 1949; *Post*, January 13, 1954.

107. *Post*, January 13, 1954.

108. Ibid., November 29, 1953; June 19, 1955; September 27, 1955.

109. *Cervi's*, November 17, 1949.

Chapter 7

110. Zeckendorf, *Autobiography*, 107, 122.

111. Caro, *Power Broker*, 772–73; Zeckendorf, "New Cities for Old," 32–34; *Post*, February 6, 1966, "Empire" magazine.

112. Zeckendorf, *Autobiography*, 108–9; *Post*, December 26, 1933.

113. *News*, May 11, 1945; June 15, 1945.

114. *Republican*, November 24, 1912.

115. *News*, December 27, 1946; *Post*, June 21, 1945; December 28, 1946; May 3, 1948; October 15, 1948.

116. *News*, January 8, 1950; January 23, 1955.

117. *News*, December 4, 1949; *Post*, December 28, 1946; January 8, 1952.

118. *Post*, February 6, 1966, "Empire" magazine.

119. *Post*, April 8, 1953; July 7, 1953; December 17, 1953.

120. *Cervi's*, July 26, 1956; *Post*, January 23, 1954; June 20, 1954.

121. *Cervi's*, July 5, 1956.

122. *News*, January 23, 1955; *Post*, January 23, 1955.

123. Zeckendorf, *Autobiography*, 125; *Cervi's*, October 19, 1957.

124. *Cervi's*, October 10, 1957, 1.

125. Ibid., December 5, 1957, 2.

126. May-D&F advertisement, *Post*, July 27, 1958.

127. *Post*, July 14, 1958.

128. *News*, August 5, 1958; *Post*, August 3, 1958; August 4, 1958.

129. Author's conversation with Bob Rhodes, October 31, 2014.

130. This section heading paraphrases General Douglas MacArthur's famous line about "old soldiers." When Zeckendorf was chairman of the board of trustees of Long Island University, the school presented MacArthur with an honorary decree.

131. Zeckendorf, *Autobiography*, 136; *Post*, February 6, 1966, "Empire" magazine.

132. *Post*, February 6, 1966, "Empire" magazine.

133. *News*, April 8, 1960.

Chapter 8

134. Fashion designer Adele Simpson, quoted in May-D&F advertisement, *News*, March 1, 1960.

135. *Post*, Advertisement, August 1, 1958.

136. Author's conversations with Bob Rhodes, October 31, 2014, and November 21, 2014. After leaving May-D&F in the mid-1970s, Rhodes purchased Denver's Evergreen Specialty Company, which contracted with major stores, hotels and office buildings across the country for holiday decorations.

137. Marcus, *Minding the Store*, 206.

138. Clipping file in Mary Fitzgerald papers, *News* (no date given).

139. "May-D&F Fortnights," notes in the files of Bob Rhodes; author's conversation with Bob Rhodes, October 31, 2014; *Post*, July 22, 1962; October 29, 1962.

140. "May-D&F Fortnights"; "The Wonderful World of Winter" notes in the files of Bob Rhodes; flyer, "The Ski Chalet on 16th Street," in the files of Bob Rhodes; *News* and *Post* clippings in files of Bob Rhodes (no dates given); *Post*, November 8, 1964; November 9, 1964.

141. "May-D&F Fortnights"; *News* and *Post* clippings in the files of Bob Rhodes (no dates given); *News*, October 23, 1966.

142. "May-D&F Fortnights"; *News*, October 18, 1968, 71; *Post*, October 21, 1968, 27.

143. http://www.lego.com/en-us/aboutus/lego-group/the_lego_history/1960, accessed April 4, 2015.

144. "May-D&F Fortnights."
145. Ibid; script for Odyssey East slideshow in the files of Bob Rhodes.
146. "May-D&F News" employee newsletter, October, 1969.
147. *News*, October 9, 1981.
148. Ibid., April 29, 1972; *Post*, June 21, 1964; February 21, 1965; April 4, 1965, "Roundup" magazine; March 27, 1966, "Empire" magazine; April 14, 1968, "Empire" magazine.
149. *News*, March 2, 1976; February 25, 1977, "Center" section; February 12, 1978, "Marathon" section; February 18, 1983, "Weekend"; *Post*, February 17, 1974, "Roundup" magazine; February 22, 1976, "Roundup" magazine; February 25, 1977; February 11, 1979, "Roundup" magazine; *Westword*, March 16, 1979.

Chapter 9

150. May Department Stores president Thomas A. Hays, in *News*, January 29, 1993.
151. *Post*, November 25, 1977.
152. *Denver Downtowner*, March 24, 1982; *News*, February 13, 1982; February 17, 1982.
153. *News*, November 14, 1984; November 18, 1984.
154. Ibid., June 23, 1986; June 26, 1986; *Post*, June 23, 1986; June 24, 1986; July 17, 1986.
155. *News*, July 17, 1987; February 18, 1987; February 19, 1987; March 4, 1987; *Post*, January 31, 1987.
156. *News*, February 20, 1987; March 4, 1987; *Post*, January 31, 1987.
157. *Post*, June 22, 1989; *News*, February 10, 1987; February 18, 1987; November 11, 1988; June 22, 1989.
158. *Denver Business Journal*, September 11, 1989; *News*, June 28, 1990.
159. *News*, February 2, 1991; February 27, 1991.
160. Ibid., March 6, 1984; December 14, 1984; August 25, 1989; September 17, 1989.
161. Ibid., January 29, 1993.
162. Ibid.
163. Ibid., April 13, 1993; April 28, 1993; July 24, 1993.
164. Press release, "Federated and May Announce Merger: $17 billion transaction to create value for customers, shareholders"; Federated Department Stores, Inc., February 28, 2005.

Epilogue

165. Alan Golin Gass, FAIA, "Who Was Bill Zeckendorf?" presentation at "Historic Denver Week" at the Denver Central Library, May 16, 1995, revised for University of Denver's VIVA! Education Series, January 29, 2004.

166. *Cervi's*, December 31, 1958, 1; *Post*, January 10, 1959; June 7, 1960.

167. *News*, October 25, 1959; *Post*, October 25, 1959; May 16, 1963; July 7, 1965; June 1, 1969.

168. *News*, March 13, 1955; August 8, 1958; *Post*, February 9, 1958; August 1, 1958; January 18, 1959.

169. *News*, June 6, 1959, 13; *Post*, December 21, 1959, 17.

170. *News*, November 1, 1961; *Post*, October 7, 1960.

171. *News*, January 17, 1961; January 27, 1961; *Post*, December 20, 1960; July 1, 1963; September 19, 1965.

172. *Cervi's*, October 5, 1966, 3; *News*, September 23, 1965; *Post*, July 29, 1965.

173. *Herald*, October 1, 1965.

174. *Cervi's*, December 14, 1966, 1, 2; *News*, November 23, 1967; *Post*, January 20, 1967; February 17, 1967; June 25, 1967; October 2, 1967; August 9, 1970.

175. *News*, November 19, 1968, 39; *Post*, April 11, 1969, 21; December 7, 1969, 1; March 18, 1970, 21.

176. *News*, July 19, 1970; January 9, 1971; *Post*, April 4, 1971.

177. *News*, January 24, 1973; *Post*, April 29, 1971; January 27, 1972; August 30, 1973; January 24, 1974.

178. *Post*, August 9, 1973; November 21, 1974.

179. *News*, August 15, 1975; *Post*, January 17, 1975; September 4, 1975; November 19, 1975.

180. *News*, March 29, 1978; *Post*, December 1, 1977; March 16, 1978; September 21, 1978; March 11, 1979.

181. *News*, December 19, 1979; February 17, 1981; *Post*, January 18, 1979; January 20, 1980.

182. Author's conversation with Richard Hentzell, June 10, 2015. The replacement doors came from the former Ford Motor Company headquarters in Dearborn, Michigan.

183. *News*, August 23, 1994.

184. Ibid., December 1, 1994.

185. Ibid., December 20, 1994; December 23, 1994.

186. Mary Voelz Chandler, "Politeness May Return to Bite Paraboloid Preservationists," *News*, Spotlight; Michael Paglia, "Zeckendorf Follies,"

Westword, May 17, 1995; Gass, "Who Was Bill Zeckendorf?"; conversation between author and Gass, May 1, 2015.

187. Michael Paglia, "Death of a Salesroom," *Westword*, August 8, 1996.

188. Gass, "Who Was Bill Zeckendorf?"

189. *News*, October 20, 1995; Paglia, "Death of a Salesroom."

190. Chandler, "Banality Mars Adam's Mark Hotel," *News*, August 31, 1997; Paglia, "Death of a Salesroom."

BIBLIOGRAPHY

Books

Barth, Gunther. *City People: The Rise of Modern City Culture in Nineteenth-Century America.* New York: Oxford University Press, 1980 (paperback edition, 1982).

Caro, Robert. *The Power Broker: Robert Moses and the Fall of New York.* New York: Alfred A. Knopf, 1974 (paperback edition New York, NY: Vintage, 1975).

Gravenhorst, Edna Campos. *Famous-Barr: St. Louis Shopping at Its Finest.* Charleston, SC: The History Press, 2014.

Johnson, Charlie H. *The Daniels & Fisher Tower.* Denver, CO: Tower Press, 1977.

Leonard, Stephen J., and Thomas J. Noel. *Denver: Mining Camp to Metropolis.* Niwot, CO: University Press of Colorado, 1990.

Marcus, Stanley. *Minding the Store.* Denton, TX: University of North Texas Press, 1997 (facsimile edition; originally published Boston, MA: Little, Brown, 1974).

Parkhill, Forbes. *Donna Madixxa Goes West: The Biography of a Witch.* Boulder, CO: Pruett Press, Inc., 1968.

Soucek, Gayle. *Marshall Field's: The Store that Helped Build Chicago.* Charleston, SC: The History Press, 2010.

Zeckendorf, William, with Edward McCreary. *The Autobiography of William Zeckendorf.* New York: Holt, Rinehart and Winston, 1970.

Other Material

Daniels and Fisher Stores Company. *From Prairie Days to 1907: Being a History of the Daniels & Fisher Stores Company*. Denver, CO: Press of the Smith-Brooks Company, 1907 (booklet).

Zeckendorf, William. "Baked Buildings," *The Atlantic*, December 1951, 46–49.

———. "New Cities for Old," *The Atlantic*, November 1951, 31–35.

INDEX

ABOUT THE AUTHOR

Photo by Heather Ormsby.

Denver native Mark A. Barnhouse has been fascinated by the city's downtown and its historic department stores from an early age. He chose Denver's Sixteenth Street as a research topic for a college paper and has been researching and writing about it ever since, along with other Denver historical subjects. He is the author of *Denver's Sixteenth Street*, *Northwest Denver* and *Lost Denver*, all available from Arcadia Publishing.